20 ADS THAT SHOOK THE WORLD

ALSO BY JAMES B. TWITCHELL

Adcult USA: The Triumph of Advertising in American Culture

Carnival Culture: The Trashing of Taste in America

For Shame: The Loss of Common Decency in American Culture

Lead Us Into Temptation: The Triumph of American Materialism

20
ADS
THAT
SHOOK
THE
WORLD

**THE CENTURY'S MOST GROUNDBREAKING ADVERTISING
AND HOW IT CHANGED US ALL**

JAMES B. TWITCHELL

CROWN PUBLISHERS / NEW YORK

Published by Crown Publishers,
201 East 50th Street, New York, New York 10022.
Member of the Crown Publishing Group.

Random House, Inc. New York, Toronto, London, Sydney, Auckland
www.randomhouse.com

CROWN is a trademark and the Crown colophon
is a registered trademark of Random House, Inc.

Manufactured in the United States of America

DESIGN BY KAREN MINSTER

Library of Congress Cataloging-in-Publication Data
Twitchell, James B., 1943–
Twenty ads that shook the world:
the century's most groundbreaking advertising
and how it changed us all / James B. Twitchell.
Includes bibliographical references.
1. Advertising. I. Title.
HF5811.T9 2000
659.1–dc21   99-42477
CIP

ISBN 0-609-60563-1

10   9   8   7   6   5   4   3   2   1

First Edition

For Mary

CONTENTS

Introduction 1

1 P. T. BARNUM: Prince of Humbug 16

2 LYDIA E. PINKHAM'S VEGETABLE COMPOUND: Personalizing the Corporate Face 26

3 PEARS' SOAP: John E. Millais's *A Child's World* and the Powers of Associated Value 38

4 PEPSODENT: Claude Hopkins and the Magic of the Preemptive Claim 48

5 LISTERINE: Gerard Lambert and Selling the Need 60

6 THE QUEENSBORO CORPORATION: Advertising on the First Electronic Medium 70

7 THE KID IN UPPER 4: The Birth of Advocacy Advertising 80

8 DE BEERS: A Good Campaign Is Forever 88

9 COKE AND CHRISTMAS: The Claus That Refreshes 102

10 THE VOLKSWAGEN BEETLE: William Bernbach and the Fourth Wall 108

11 MISS CLAIROL'S "DOES SHE ... OR DOESN'T SHE?": How to Advertise a Dangerous Product 118

12 THE MARLBORO MAN: The Perfect Campaign 126

13 THE HATHAWAY MAN: David Ogilvy and the Branding of Branding 136

14 ANACIN AND THE UNIQUE SELLING PROPOSAL: How Would You Like a Hammer in the Head? 146

15 LBJ VS. BARRY GOLDWATER: Thirty-Second Politics 154

16 SHE'S VERY CHARLIE: The Politics of Scent 162

17 ABSOLUT: The Metaphysics of Wrap 174

18 APPLE'S *1984:* The Ad as Artifact 184

19 THE RISE AND FALL AND RISE OF THE INFOMERCIAL: "Call Now! Operators Are Standing By ..." 194

20 NIKE AND MICHAEL JORDAN: The Hero as Product 204

Works Cited 217
Index 221

INTRODUCTION

Ads, The Sponsored Art of Capitalism

Commercial speech—advertising—makes up most of what we share as a culture. No one is happy about this, not even the people who make it. They call it clutter, which is rather like a doctor complaining about a frantic patient after he has shot him full of adrenaline. The rest of us call the current glut of advertising by worse names. But, call it what you will, language about products and services has pretty much replaced language about all other subjects. And it's not going away.

As the language of commercialism has become louder, the language of high culture has become quieter; it seems to be ending not with a bang, but with a whimper. We all know the funereal refrain: The canon of recognized literary works, the shared vocabulary of known lines, our cultural literacy, the wink-wink of allusions to hundreds of years of "the best that has been thought and said" has all but disappeared thanks to "a few words from the sponsor."

Ask anyone under the age of fifty to fill in the blank in what was arguably the most famous line in nineteenth-century poetry, Wordsworth's "My heart leaps up when I behold a ... in the sky." Few can do it (it's "rainbow" in case you're wondering). But ask the same group what's in a Big Mac and you'll hear, "Two all-beef patties, special sauce, lettuce, cheese, pickles, and onions on a sesame-seed bun." It's sad to say that more of us know Morris the cat than William Morris, and more about Mr. Whipple and Mr. Clean than about Mr. Kurtz and Mrs. Dalloway.

Commercial culture, the putative enemy of high culture, is currently in a period

1

of rapid ascendancy. And for good reason. While we older people may laud what we take to be "monuments of unaging intellect," while we may support our local PBS affiliate, while we may act distressed at the plight of the National Endowments, our concern really makes no difference. Commercialism is here to stay, delivering the goods to those with the time and money to consume them.

Generation X is the first generation to know the world almost entirely through commercialism. A *New Yorker* cartoon of a few years ago has a father saying to his small son while looking up at a rainbow: "It isn't advertising *anything*, dammit." Even baby boomers have been profoundly affected. Remember the telling scene in the film *Saturday Night Fever* in which a character mentions Laurence Olivier to John Travolta, who's never heard of him. "He's the great actor," the friend says. "Never heard of him," Travolta mumbles. "Come on," the friend says, "the guy in the Polaroid commercials." "Oh yeah, him."

In 1915 it was perfectly possible to go entire weeks without observing an ad. When I was growing up in the 1950s, just as television was entering the bloodstream, ads were confined to distinct "pods," and everyone knew where they were. No longer. The average young adult today sees some 5,000 ads each day, in almost every minute, in almost every place. The only ad-free refuge is sleep and prayer.

Put simply, it's hard to understand a culture that has outposts in your mind. It's hard to criticize commercialism while humming a mindless jingle for chewing gum that has something to do with gleefully happy twins doubling pleasure; while worrying about halitosis, dandruff, and water spots; while trying to decide among the thirty-seven different kinds of toothpaste; while buying outrageously overpriced sneakers with big check marks on them; while eating something called "Real Turkey Pastrami," "I Can't Believe It's Not Butter," "This Can't Be Yogurt," and, well, you get the point. This stuff is the water. We are the fish.

Advertising has become the dominant culture, yet what an irony that we know so much about specific advertisements, so little about advertising as a form of persuasion, and almost nothing about the history of selling. This phenomenon is not limited to consumers. In fact, if you really want to observe the paradox, ask an adman.

Ask someone in advertising about some famous relationship like John E. Powers and Wanamaker's department store, in which the copywriter insisted on telling the unvarnished truth; about some over-the-top campaign like Scott Toilet Tissue in the 1930s, in which surgery is the implied alternative to proper hygiene; about some great insight, like the genius who suggested that Alka-Seltzer drop two tablets into the glass instead of one and hence doubled the sales; about some ad-based cultural transformation, like calling payouts-at-death "life insurance," and chances are you will be met with a blank stare.

Now ask a doctor about the development of blood transfusions, ask a lawyer about railroads and tort law, ask an English professor about how Shakespeare was rewritten in the eighteenth century. Why do they have institutional memories while admen don't?

To some degree this collective amnesia stems from how all of us look at advertising. At first glance, it is self-evidently disposable, and therefore not worthy of study. It is, in a word, trash. And, as well, when one looks back at ads they seem hopelessly dated and often ineffectual. Let's face it, advertising today is all about being current, or even ahead of the curve. So why look at what is behind the times?

Could our neglect also be because people in marketing are slightly ashamed of what they do, and hence don't want to know what's come before? After all, if the people practicing your trade have been regularly excoriated, maybe you, too, would want to stay blissfully ignorant of your history. Or do salesmen think that advertising is so evolved that they only need to know what's happening right now so they can copy it? That certainly might explain why so much modern advertising is unflaggingly derivative and uninspired. Or is it because advertising has become so much of our culture that we think that it has no history? Anthropologists tell us that if fish could think, the last thing they would think about was water.

Certainly part of the reason people in sales are so untethered to their own cultural history is that advertising courses in universities cover almost everything except the past. When I've asked people who teach advertising why this is, they say it's because the accrediting process discourages everything but hands-on experience. The advertising faculty see themselves as part of a technical school where they teach a journeyman trade, rather than as part of a professional school where they teach the art and history of persuasion. Advertising is taught in the schools of journalism and business, not in liberal arts and sciences.

So I want to address the problem of an incomplete education not just for practitioners, but for all students of popular culture. Like it or not, Marshall McLuhan was not too far off when he rather grandly said that advertising has become "the greatest *art* form of the twentieth century." It certainly merits more than the arched eyebrows and tsk-tsks it usually receives. Believe it or not, great advertising is also an *intellectual* enterprise. Little is haphazard about it, although it often seems so casual, often whimsical, even *anti*-intellectual.

A Tradition of Advertising

There are many ways to decode commercial speech; in this book I will be using a kind of art-historical approach in which the artifact of the ad is the basis of interpretation. What makes it work? What's the story behind it? How did it change the way we looked not just at the advertised object, but at other things as well?

It would be comforting if the instances I have chosen led to some crescendo of understanding. But what one finds is that great ads are not always congruent with each other, nor do they progress to higher and higher sophistication. Some of the best are very crude, and some of the worst are very sophisticated. But when you think about it, isn't this also true with works of literature, music, and painting?

Although some may regard the comparison as sacrilegious, I take the twenty ads examined in this book as analogous to those touchstone works of high culture that F. R. Leavis called the Great Tradition. These ads are like what in medieval times were known as *sententiae*, those passages of theological matter that could be expanded and contracted, but not pushed aside. These are the clichés of commercialism, the central passages of words and images that won't go away, although they only stay before our eyes for a few seconds. They often are, in a sense, inspired. We know them even if we haven't seen them, because our culture has been built around them.

As opposed to literature and theology, advertising sets itself up for a shoot-from-the-hip exegesis. Ads are made to be consumed on the run, piled one on top of another. Although they come to us in pictures and text, they are like background music. We hear them without listening. They have become, as Jack Kroll wrote in *Newsweek* a quarter of a century ago, "the most pervasive music in the history of—er, civilization" (Kroll 1975, 69).

While agencies may claim to clients that they can create desires, ads can only strike occasional chords, and only then for an instant. Or, to change the sensation, advertising does its work in the wink of an eye. Stephen Leacock, the English humorist, once said that advertising is "the science of arresting the human intelligence just long enough to get money from it" (Jackman 1982, 1).

The waste in generating such short-lived ephemera is huge and is the understandable object of much criticism. While we may see and hear thousands of ads each day, only two or three ever get remembered, and only a few of those ever lead to a purchase. Fewer still ever work their way into our nervous systems. Video Storyboard

Tests reports that a startling 40 percent of the 20,000 consumers surveyed each year cannot think of a single "memorable" commercial. But we don't have to buy a product, or even remember an ad, to consume advertising. That comes to us, whether we like it or not, "free of charge."

If art struggles to create images of eternity, ads settle for what's happening right now. Advertising is the big-print edition of the Rosetta Stone, modern cave art in strobe lights. But don't sell it short. The legendary adman Earnest Elmo Calkins was certainly correct when he wrote of advertisements: "These humbler adjuncts to literature may prove more valuable to the future historian than the editorial contents. In them we may trace our sociological history, the rise and fall of fads and crazes, changing interests and changing tastes, in food and clothes, amusements and vices, a panorama of life as it was lived, more informing than old diaries and crumbling tombstones" (Calkins 1946, 222–30).

A number of lists of ads already exist, and I have been helped by thinking about them. Although every multinational agency has a reel of what it takes to be its best work, in 1995 the Global Product Committee of the Leo Burnett Company put together a tape of what it takes to be the "100 Best Television Commercials of All Time," which is the basis of Bernice Kanner's *The 100 Best TV Commercials*. There have been books of lists compiled by practitioners: *The 100 Greatest Advertisements* (1949; revised 1959), by Julian Lewis Watkins, who had spent his life in the business, and *100 Top Copy Writers and Their Favorite Ads* (1954), assembled by the editors of *Printer's Ink*, a trade journal. For its Bicentennial Collection (April 19, 1976), *Advertising Age* asked a distinguished panel of ninety-seven admen and three adwomen to list "the best ads or ad campaigns that you've ever seen or heard" and published the result. And for its special issue on "The Advertising Century" (1999), Bob Garfield ranked the top one hundred advertising campaigns. *Entertainment*

Weekly, which loves lists, dedicated an entire issue (March 28, 1997) to anointing "the fifty greatest commercials of all time." And true to its role as the *vade mecum* of the industry, *Advertising Age* now maintains a lively Web site (adage.com) listing the fifty best commercials over the last fifty years, dividing them by decades.

But my list is different. I am after the most *profound* ads ever produced. Not profound in the sense of being clever, or in the sense of selling product, but in the sense of being like a poem, like a painting, like a series of musical notes, deep and moving, axiomatic. What were the ads that became part of the nervous system, became part of the lingua franca? Which ads really had the beef?

Advertising of this sort is more like Renaissance art than modern art. In the Renaissance, painters like Michelangelo, Leonardo, and Giotto did not paint what they wanted to paint. They were usually told exactly what to paint, and even how to paint it. Then they were told to paint it again, just a little differently. Their clients were the mendicant orders of the Roman Catholic Church. Although the corporate headquarters was in Rome, the individual orders had some say in how they chose their advertising (what we now call art). Competition among these orders produced some of the greatest creations of the Western imagination, in part because they never forgot (or never were allowed to forget) the necessity of drawing an audience by addressing its deepest needs.

Now I'm not saying that cathedrals are billboards, or that frescoes are thirty-second spots, but there are similarities too important to overlook.

Modern art, however, is different. Here the artist is working for himself and he is rewarded for breaking boundaries, for getting out of line, for being shocking with the New, taking liberties. Think of all the movements of modern art—Cubism, Abstract Expressionism, Impressionism—and you will see that creativity often means violently disturbing expectations. It gets attention not for what it says, but for how it says it.

My list is of Renaissance ads, not modern ones. When I hear the term "breakthrough" or "cutting edge" used in advertising, I realize something forgettable is about to happen. From my vantage point as a cultural historian, part of the reason there is so much clutter in advertising today is that copywriters and art directors struggle more to "get through" than to "make a point." Almost all advertising that wins such annual prizes as Clios, Effies, and Addies is modern advertising of this sort. When it comes to this kind of creativity, the famous quotation (attributed to both John Wanamaker and Lord Leverhume) that "half my advertising dollars are wasted—I just can't figure out which half" needs to have the percent of waste increased.

Essentially, therefore, I want to treat these keystone print and television advertisements the way Cleanth Brooks and Robert Penn Warren treated individual poems in the 1940s, as objects deserving of formal readings. In their *Understanding Poetry,* the critics made the then-radical claim that certain poems were especially rich in meanings, that these poems were concentrated moments of human attention, and that when they "worked" they gave us lasting insight into the human condition. In this sense, they were truly creative.

The ads I have chosen may not make you gulp, but they did change the way we swallowed information about the world around us. They got into our bloodstreams. Many of the products are no longer produced, which raises the interesting question of exactly how important advertising really is. Some of the ads take totally different approaches, which raises the intriguing question of the nature of human desire. Maybe there is a lot more going on in consumption than exploiting anxiety, "keeping up with the Joneses," or consuming conspicuously. Maybe consumption can be liberating, a way to construct the self. And some of the ads I've chosen seem so pedestrian to us now, sometimes downright embarrassing, which may only testify to how completely we have assimilated their content.

More telling, I think, is that the great creative ads always seem so easy to create.

This is deceptive. They only *seem* simple. As Aldous Huxley said, almost anyone can write a passable sonnet, but composing a good ad is tough. A good ad never seems to be what it really is, namely an attempt to get under your radar and drop a little bomb. And as Huxley's contemporary George Orwell observed, while all art is propaganda, all propaganda is not necessarily art. To me, these twenty ads are propaganda achieving the condition of popular art.

The Power of Advertising

In 1917 John Reed wrote *Ten Days That Shook the World,* a book based on his experience observing the Bolshevik Revolution. It created quite a stir, especially among intellectuals. A few years ago Warren Beatty's movie *Reds* resuscitated Mr. Reed for a brief time. Reed's story is compelling because he was so certain that he had seen the future. The future of the West would depend on bloody political events that were moving rapidly through the Eurasian marketplace of ideas. The workers would rule the world. It was all but inevitable, dialectical, done. Capitalism was to be history. Advertising would evaporate as "use" value would push "concocted" value aside. In the utopian workers' paradise, nothing would come between human beings and their necessary objects.

Reed was wrong. Of all the -isms of our century, none has proved more successful than the one that underlies all political systems—materialism. It is our love of *stuff,* of having things, of trading and hoarding, of buying and selling, even of talking about things, that makes modern political systems possible. Until the nineteenth century, only the aristocracy could traffic in extraneous things. The special things they consumed even had a distinct category name. They were luxuries, things that shone, *de luxe.*

With the rise of the Industrial Revolution, however, the rest of us had a go at them. While we might not have been able to have the same brand of object as the nobility, we could certainly have a version of it—a Ford if not a Cadillac. Use value in such a system became less important than prestige value or what Marx called exchange value. We started to find most of life's meanings in having and displaying these special things. They became heraldic crests, coats of arms, badges, bloodlines. Consumption became conspicuous because that was how we differentiated ourselves.

What we often forget is that it is our love of consuming things once considered beyond our means that caused the great machine age, that rewarded us for applying water, steam, and electricity to the engines of production to make them still more efficient and, in so doing, turn luxuries into necessities, wants into needs. We fool ourselves to think that machine production *caused* materialism. How much more accurate to acknowledge that it was our desire for distinctive things that led to the explosion of machine production.

In a sense, the politics of the twentieth century has been an attempt to figure out how to distribute efficiently the surplus goods of a machine production. Little wonder that the workers of the world wanted to unite. They would get to those surpluses. But what the Marxists didn't appreciate was that we were not made materialistic by machine power; rather, it was machine power that was made by our materialism.

Machine-made stuff is problematic for one simple reason: it is all so similar. Economists call such objects *fungible* because they are interchangeable, homogeneous. Advertisers call them *parity items.* If my machine works just like yours, then what it produces will be interchangeable with yours. If a producer is not careful, he'll have to eat his surplus. So not only does he make similar things, but he also has to make his products *seem* different.

What we really crave is not just material, but material with meaning. The process of instilling meaning into machine-made goods is called commercialism. Advertising is at the heart of commercialism. It is the part that adds the meaning and, in so doing, attempts to make one identical object more valuable than another. The great adman Rosser Reeves used to illustrate this. He would hold up two quarters and then, pointing to one of them, say, "My job is to make you think that *this* quarter is more valuable than *that* one."

Commercialism involves two processes: *commodification,* or the stripping of an object of all other values except its value for sale to someone else; and *marketing,* the insertion of the object into a network of exchanges only some of which involve money. Until the 1850s, commercialization was pretty well limited to commodification, since large-volume market networks scarcely existed throughout much of Europe. But with the creation of the first European colonial empires, and even more with the creation of mass industrial production, cheap transportation, and communications, the marketing of commodities took on a relentless life of its own.

Marketing and its subset, advertising, should not be nasty words. Religions have been doing it for generations. If you like it, it is called saving souls; if you don't, it is called proselytizing. Religions tend to make this world meaningful by creating value in the next. Commercialism, more specifically advertising, does precisely that to the fungible objects of the here and now.

The pressure to commercialize—to turn things into commodities and then market them—has been particularly Western. As Max Weber first argued in *The Protestant Ethic and the Spirit of Capitalism* (1905), much of the Protestant Reformation was geared toward denying the holiness of many things that the church had endowed with meanings. From the inviolable priesthood to the sacrificial holy water, this secularizing movement systematically unloaded meaning. Soon the marketplace would capture this offloaded meaning and apply it to machine-made things.

You can still see the religious roots of commercialism in advertising. Buy this object and you'll be saved. You deserve a break today. You, you're the one. We are the company that cares about you. You are in good hands. We care. Trust in us. Buy now.

If you recognize some of the twenty ads that follow—and you will—it is because they are part of what we share. They are the world wrought not by religion or science or art. They are the world wrought by advertising. They are pushed our way by a culture "on the take."

We all know the world populated by Madge, Mr. Whipple, and Colonel Sanders: a world in which cats and dogs sing into microphones about their dinner choices; in which raisins dance and household bugs spill their guts; in which Mrs. Olsen, a giant green man in a scarf, cookie elves, and a white knight on horseback riding through our backyard with a lance can be trusted; in which "Because I'm worth it," "You deserve a break today," "Be all that you can be," "We try harder," or "Quality is Job 1" are taken at face value; in which we can feel "really clean"; in which various tigers are telling us what to put into our cereal bowls and into our gas tanks; in which we can't do simple math but know what is $99^{44}/_{100}$ percent pure, what has 57 varieties, and the importance of a cigarette being a "silly millimeter" longer than others; a world in which we are encouraged to be a Pepper, to teach the world to sing, and to become an "uncola nut" all at the same time; a world in which we all know the same double entendres: flick your Bic, take it all off, a little dab'll do ya. It is a world of feigned sincerity, eternal optimism, and lots and lots and lots of small problems and difficult moments that we can master. And it is powerful. More people report crying over a greeting card company's advertising than over any other regularly televised event.

As much as this world has been pushed at us, it has been pulled in by us. This wafer-thin world has come between us and mass-produced things not because we are too materialistic, but because we are not materialistic enough. If we craved objects *and* knew what they meant, there would be no need to add meaning through advertising. We would just gather, use, toss out, or hoard indiscriminately. But we don't.

First, we don't know what to gather; second, we like to trade what we have gathered; and, third, we need to know how to value objects that have little practical use. What is clear is that most things in and of themselves do not mean enough. In fact, what we crave may not be objects at all but their meaning. For whatever else advertising "does," one thing is certain: by adding value to material, by adding meaning to objects, by branding things, advertising performs a role historically associated with religion. Salvation awaits not in the next world but in the next aisle. No wonder early department stores were referred to as "cathedrals of consumption." Like it or not, the canon of received wisdom lies in understanding these strange bits of commercial speech, for indeed this is the stuff that has shaken the world.

My contention in this book will seem counterintuitive at first, given the clamor of our times against commercialism, but here it is: I believe that, paradoxically, we have not grown weaker but stronger by accepting these self-evidently ridiculous myths that sacramentalize mass-produced interchangeable objects. We have not wasted away, but have proved more powerful, have not devolved and been rebarbarized, but seem to have marginally improved the physical condition of being on this planet. Dreaded consumption (note the connection of this word with the AIDS of Victorian life, namely tuberculosis) and the vast wasteland of media babble notwithstanding, commercialism has lessened pain. Most of us have more pleasure and less discomfort in our lives than most of the people most of the time in all of history. Little wonder that people all over the world are clamoring for what we have, including our advertising.

As awful as it may seem, when young people around the world are asked what freedom means, most of them say the freedom to buy what you want, when you want it, and to use it how you want. Although we don't usually admit it, this was at the heart of our own American Revolution. Recall the Boston Tea Party. We did not like to be told what to buy and how much to pay for it. As de Tocqueville observed almost two centuries ago, advertising worked well in America as it appealed to our "love of material gratification." Now the rest of the world is having a go at it.

Historian Daniel Boorstin has said that Europeans used to go to market to get what they want, whereas Americans go to market to *discover* what they want. In the developed world, we are all Americans now, and the market comes to all consumers, via advertising.

While we all admit that the pen is mightier than the sword, it is hard to acknowledge that in our century the pen is more likely in the hands of some copywriter extolling the virtues of a nicotine delivery system to children than wielded by some passionate revolutionary exhorting the freedom of expression for the oppressed and downtrodden.

But hard as it may be to defend this often vulgar and sometimes amoral culture of getting and spending, it does not hurt to try to understand it. In many respects, commercialism is indeed, as adman George Lois fatuously boasted, "poison gas." It surrounds objects, being pumped *and* drawn everywhere, into the farthest reaches of space and into the smallest divisions of time. In a less toxic analogy, commercialism is like smoke in a wind tunnel of machine-made things. The fan is never turned off.

By no means am I sanguine about a culture in which advertising gauges value and sets standards. On Madison Avenue it is often said that we consume the advertising not the product, that we drink the commercial not the beer, drive the nameplate not the car, smoke the jingle not the cigarette. There is no doubt that such a system is wasteful; devoid of otherworldly concerns, it lives for today and celebrates the body. It may well overindulge and spoil the young with impossible promises and few demands. It certainly encourages recklessness, living beyond one's means, gambling. Consumer culture is always new and improved, always bigger and better, always loud, always without a past and with a perpetually rosy future. Again, like religion, which in many ways it has displaced, it afflicts the comfortable and comforts the afflicted. It is a one-dimensional world, a micron-thin world, a world low on significance and high on shine.

But you might also realize that while you don't have to like it, or even buy into it, you need to understand our part in its history. Almost a decade ago, Francis Fukuyama contended in his controversial "The End of History?" essay (and later book) that "the ineluctable spread of consumerist Western culture" presages "not just the end of the Cold War, or the passing of a particular period of postwar history, but the end of history as such: that is, the end point of mankind's ideological evolution" (Fukuyama 1989, 3–4).

Such predictions are not new. "The End of History" (as we know it) and the "end point of mankind's ideological evolution" have been predicted before by philosophers. Hegel claimed it had already happened in 1806 when Napoleon embodied the ideals of the French Revolution, and Marx said the end was coming soon with world communism. What legitimizes this modern claim is that it is demonstrably true. For better or for worse, American commercial culture is well on its way to becoming world culture. And these twenty ads are important milestones along the way.

Let's also admit that, much as we love to blame advertising, *it* has not led us astray. Ads "R" Us. The idea that advertising creates artificial desires rests on a wistful ignorance of history and human nature, on the hazy, romantic feeling that there existed some halcyon era of noble savages with purely natural needs. Once we are fed and sheltered, our needs are and have always been cultural, not natural. Until there is some other system to codify and satisfy those needs and yearnings, commercialism— and the culture it carries with it—will continue not just to thrive but to triumph.

1

P. T. BARNUM

Prince of Humbug

IF AMERICAN LITERATURE, as Ernest Hemingway said, starts with Mark Twain's *Huckleberry Finn*, then American advertising starts with P. T. Barnum's masterful deceptions. Barnum knew how to turn Dr. Samuel Johnson's famous definition of advertising— "promise, large promise"—into words and images that still capture attention. William Lyon Phelps, a Yale professor of English in the 1930s and host of a vastly popular radio show, knew what he was saying when he called Barnum "the Shakespeare of advertising."

If you watch enough late-night commercials on television, listen to enough ads on your car radio, open enough junk mail, and peruse your share of ads in newspapers and magazines, then you realize that the spirit of P. T. Barnum lives on. When you hear, "Don't miss this once-in-a-lifetime opportunity," "Limited edition collector's item at an unbelievably low special discount price," or "Going out of business, last and final liquidation closeout sale! All items must go! We're closing our doors forever! Even longer than that! This is it! Absolutely! You can't afford to miss it!" you are hearing Barnum.

Just as we attribute lines to Shakespeare that are nowhere to be found in his works, so, too, Barnum has achieved the accolade of shadow authorship. If he didn't write it, he should have. Barnum is the author in spirit, but not in fact, of such great marketing quips as

There's a sucker born every minute.

You can fool most of the people most of the time.

Never overestimate the taste of the American public.

LOOK FOR IT! WAIT FOR IT!

☞ SEE IT!! ☜

It is Coming

In its Overwhelming Preponderance over any other Show in Existence.

P.T. BARNUM'S

OWN AND ONLY

I AM COMING!

I AM COMING!

GREATEST SHOW

ON EARTH!

Without a Rival, Recognizing No Equal, and Regarding No Opposition, which receives

A GRAND OVATION

From the Press and Public wherever it appears, and is universally pronounced

THE CROWNING SUCCESS

Evolved from the experience of half a century, and a long series of successful ventures in catering to the tastes of the people, and to present

A PERFECT EXHIBITION!

VAST IN ITS PROPORTIONS!
HIGH AND PURE IN TONE!
EXALTED IN ITS AIM!
VARIED IN ATTRACTIONS!
FRUITFUL OF INSTRUCTION!
The ACME of REFINED ELEGANCE
And BEST IN ALL THINGS!

This Unapproachable Model of Supreme Excellence!

WILL EXHIBIT AT

OTTAWA,

TUESDAY, AUGUST 19

Without Diminution or Curtailment in any Department, but with

LARGELY INCREASED ATTRACTIONS!

Ever offered by me in any previous year. ☞For a Partial List of its GRAND FEATURES See Other Side.

The Public's Obedient Servant.

P. T. BARNUM.

☞ REMEMBER MY DAY AND DATE, and do not confound it with any other. There is but ONE BARNUM SHOW in existence—

"The Greatest Show on Earth,"

which never fails to keep its appointments, which never disappoints the public, which gives

TEN TIMES THE WORTH OF YOUR MONEY!

And NEVER ADVERTISES anything which it DOES NOT EXHIBIT

I Am Coming:
Circus herald
for P. T. Barnum's
Greatest Show
on Earth, 1879.

However, one much-quoted remark is definitely his: "The people like to be humbugged."

In a sense, what Barnum did was to translate the everyday world of Yankee wit into commercialized guile. As a young man desperate to leave the dreary world of the family farm, he clerked in a general merchandise store near Bethel, Connecticut. Here he presided over biscuits, brandy, and Bibles, over all manner of fresh produce, hardware, and textiles, over sugar, salt, and tobacco. What these goods had in common was that they needed a little push to get them out the door. They needed a little value added, a little nudge. They were all so ordinary, so much like what you could buy in any other store.

Young Barnum reveled behind the counter. He soon realized it was what you said about an object that gave it value and distinguished it from what was in the same barrel next door. Part of the barter of exchange was that you attached your story to a product and then that's what you sold.

And nowhere did Barnum learn this better than with the product he sold best: lottery tickets. Private lotteries were common, corrupt, and thoroughly capitalistic. As an agent, he learned that you don't sell the ticket, you sell the dream. And you sell the dream by promising the future, to be sure, but also by insisting that right here, right now, is the time to buy. Barnum's lottery office soon became one of the largest suppliers of tickets in New England. "My profits," Barnum humbly reported, "were immense."

It was only a hop and a skip before he was applying exactly the same selling techniques to his new endeavors: the selling of oddities to the curious, the merchandising first of hoaxes and then of entire exhibits of the weird and dubious to an audience that prided itself on savvy. That audience was the supposedly sophisticated urbanites of the new world, New Yorkers, and his new venue was the supermarket of the strange, the commercial museum—what was to become, with the circus, the sideshow.

In 1841 Barnum purchased the building and contents of John Scudder's American Museum, a five-story firetrap on Broadway just north of the Battery. Nothing in this building was what it seemed. Everything had a story. It was a temple to Humbug. But the system was the same.

Supposedly no one complained when Barnum introduced the "inverted horse" at his museum. This "natural anomaly" had its head and tail reversed in position. The curious paid and then found an ordinary horse, tethered by its tail in its stall. His rhinoceros was advertised as a unicorn. The first hippopotamus seen in America was called "the Behemoth of the Scriptures." The public loved it.

When Barnum wanted to get people out of a crowded exhibit, he would erect a sign proclaiming "This Way to the Egress" and place it over the exit door. Customers, expecting to see some sort of exotic waterfowl, found themselves on the outside of the show, and they had to pay again to get back in. They were not mad, however, but amused.

Again like Shakespeare, Barnum's genius was so powerful that it left us a legacy of specific words that refer to events now long since forgotten. When you use the word *jumbo* to describe size, thank Barnum. In 1882 Barnum bought from Regent's Park Zoo in London a six-ton elephant named Jumbo whose name he splashed on every wall and billboard he could find. "Jumbomania" was the beginning of the contrived madness that marks modern show business. People *had* to see him. After Jumbo was accidentally killed by a train, Barnum had his skin and skeleton exhibited separately, mounted on special movable wagons and followed by Jumbo's "widow," Alice, who was trained to carry black-bordered sheets with her trunk and wipe her eyes every few steps.

And on the subject of elephants. When you refer to that polyester jumpsuit with bell-bottoms in your closet as a white elephant, you are paying tribute to the master. When a circus competitor of Barnum's brought in a white elephant from Siam, the public flocked to see it. Not to have his audience stolen, P. T. whitewashed one of his garden-variety gray elephants and advertised it so heavily that the competitor lost out. Thanks to Barnum's humbug, the authentic white elephant lost the charm and value of rarity. Even worse, his competitor couldn't sell the real white elephant because the market had collapsed.

Barnum was also the father of what today is known as event advertising or, perhaps more accurately, pseudo-event advertising. His influence can be seen in the relentless hype of movies and sporting events, "once in a lifetime" performances "not to be missed." "Must-see TV," indeed! Barnum knew that when the emphasis in Show Business is on the first word, the second word follows.

Admired for his unflagging energy and ingenuity, trashed for his brazen opportunism and "vulgarity," as *The Nation* once put it, Barnum blazed the trail for skilled self-promoters of every stripe and in every medium. And when some worn-out entertainer takes his good-bye, farewell, last-time-ever tour, remember that this, too, starts with Barnum. Whether it be an elephant going to the glue factory, or a voiceless singer going into retirement, Barnum knew that promising the last of something was almost as compelling as promising the first.

No matter what you sell, or when you sell it, Barnum knew that the first law was "You must gather a crowd." Make traffic. Then you must hold them in place. And finally, once they are calmed down, you can deliver the pitch. Anyone can attract attention with any number of pants-dropping escapades, but it is a talent to hold a large audience still and attentive. Very often what quiets them is an outrageous promise. I will show you something you have never seen before, says the carnival barker.

Want to see the bee-ootiful Mermaid from Feejee, a sight to dream of, "a bare-breasted, fish-tailed enchantress"? Thousands of people in the 1840s did. They lined up for hours outside Barnum's American Museum, as he renamed the emporium after a disastrous fire. They saw the head of a monkey crudely sewn on the body of a fish. Here, just have a look, says the advertisement for some blockbuster movie, some baldness cream, some get-rich-quick scheme, some diet pill, some way to succeed without work.... We line up and look.

When we don't like this holding action, we call it *hype*. In the nineteenth century it was called *humbug*. Humbug was part of a new lexicon that included words like *hoopla, ballyhoo, bunkum, flimflam, claptrap,* and *codswallop*. These were new words to describe a new form of uniquely American entertainment: the media-made confected event, high on promise, low on delivery, and probably costing something. As the actress Tallulah Bankhead once remarked after a rather disappointing but much-hyped evening at the theater, "There is less in this than meets the eye." This was exactly the kind of media-made event that Barnum first mastered.

Barnum was not alone in playing off the tensions between frontier bravado and urbanized conformity. In the 1830s the *New York Sun* temporarily became America's best-selling paper by publishing a fictitious story about the discovery of life on the moon. Edgar Allan Poe scammed the news world with a bogus report of a transatlantic balloon flight. This was a time when the tall tales of characters like Davy Crockett were just making the rounds. This was Barnum's milieu, and no one choreographed it better.

P. T. Barnum was the self-proclaimed Prince of Humbug. Creating it was his life's work. He spun out stories not just around the Feejee mermaid but around Joice Heath (George Washington's supposed nurse), Charles Stratton (a midget who became General Tom Thumb), Eng and Chang (the Siamese twins who fathered some twenty-two children), a microcephalic black dwarf (who was first advertised as the "What Is It?"—as the missing link between man and monkey—and later as "Zip"), the Wild Men of Borneo, and Jo-Jo the Dog-Faced Boy. Barnum knew that one could not anticipate, let alone understand, an event without a context, a frame, a story ... hype.

He knew as well that in the hands of a master, humbug became more than claptrap that you jury-rigged around your product. When it worked, what you sold was both the product and the humbug, the steak and the sizzle. As they now say on Madison Avenue, you drink the advertising right along with the beer. Which tastes better?

Barnum's most outrageous humbug, however, was himself. He was not just a self-made man (at one time the second most wealthy one living in Manhattan), but the image of a man made by himself. Long before Colonel Sanders, Lee Iacocca, Ed McMahon, and Donald Trump, the pitchman persona of Barnum was known throughout the land.

Have a look at this herald (as it was known in the circus trade) announcing the arrival of the circus. "Look for it," we are told. "It is coming." The vertical text on either side of Barnum makes clear that He is Coming. *I am Coming!* Barnum is no fool. He knew exactly what this kind of language was hyping. These words were drawn from the apocalyptic tradition of evangelical Christianity. As well, he knew exactly what he was implying when he called his circus "The Greatest Show on Earth" or "This Unapproachable Model of Supreme Excellence," or contended that it was a "crowning success." That Barnum is casting himself as the Redeemer, that he is analogizing his show to the Greatest Show in Heaven, is no happenstance. True to his reputation, Barnum is generating humbug by the ton. And this variety is just an inch short of sacrilege.

His critics knew well what he was up to. An editorial writer for *The Nation* even blasted Barnum for his effrontery: "He is the personification of a certain kind of humbug which, funny as it often appears, eats out the heart of religion" (Kunhardt et al. 1995, 201). But, as Barnum would say, you take value where you can find it.

The relationship between Christianity and advertising has often been noted. Indeed, the first generation of advertising men came from close proximity to the church. Very often they even studied for the ministry. Admen like Claude Hopkins, F. W. Ayer, Artemas Ward, James Webb Young, Theodore MacManus, and especially Bruce Barton (who went on to write *The Man Nobody Knows*, which cast Jesus as an account exec going about "my Father's business") were acutely aware of the importance of promise, of salvation, of sincerity and of all the techniques of persuasion necessary to keep the congregation paying attention.

What separated Barnum from the evangelical Elmer Gantrys was that he so gleefully attached himself to this tradition. He knew why people came to his church, as it were, and he never disappointed them. He knew the difference between attracting and duping. Of his business strategy he said, "I don't believe in duping the public, but I do believe in first *attracting* and then pleasing them." He even called his audience his "congregation," as if to make sure they got the point.

Two weeks before the circus came rolling into town, Barnum would send his advertising coach down the rails. Plastered all around this converted passenger car was his gaudy portrait surrounded by exotic animals and circus acts. Townspeople were invited to tour the coach, to see its rich appointments and marvel at its luxury. A crowd was being drawn, word of mouth was starting, hype was being spun like sugar candy.

Not only did the car advertise Barnum's "Grand Touring Museum, Menagerie, Caravan and Circus" (in that order), it also housed his advertising cadre of bill posters, plasterers, guttersnipes, press agents, and circus flacks, ready for saturation advertising. The coach itself was loaded with heralds, posters, banners, couriers, and newspaper cuts. The expense of spreading this word was one-third of all the circus expenses—some $100,000 a year in the 1870s!

Barnum was probably the first adman to understand the bizarre ratios between the spending of money on advertising and the increasing of revenues. As well, he understood the importance of creating occasions in which to make the sale. The circus was no passing happenstance; it became one of the major community events of the year. In many towns across the country, circus day was as important as the Fourth of July. In his autobiography, Barnum humbly acknowledges his contribution: "I thoroughly understood the art of advertising, not merely by means of printer's ink, which I have always used freely, and to which I confess myself much indebted for my success, but by turning every possible circumstance to my account" (Barnum 1855, 102).

After President Grant returned home from a world tour, he was dining with the great impresario. "General, since your trip you must be the best known man on the globe," Barnum commented. "By no means," the President replied. "You beat me sky-high; for where ever I went—in China, Japan, the Indies, etc.—the constant inquiry was, 'Do you know Barnum?' I think, Barnum, you are the best known man in the world." Barnum was clearly pleased. He should have been, or his advertising had been wasted. Later in life, when he took his troupe to England for a triumphal final engagement, the show would come to a stop from time to time as the old man would stand and bellow, "I suppose you all come to see Barnum. Wa-al, I'm Barnum."

Although the circus herald promised that Barnum would be appearing at Ottawa (near Chicago), such would not be the case. Barnum almost never traveled with the circus. He rarely used the gaudy railcar. Most of the time he was home in Bridgeport, Connecticut, doing what he loved best: writing circus advertising.

More than anyone else, P. T. Barnum invented what we now take to be the commercial exploitation of the human condition. His legacy includes the manufacture of hype, the conjunction of redemption and consumption, the colonization of the pseudo-event, the immediate exploitation of new media and imagery, the exchange of story for value, celebrity endorsements, the saturation of language with audacious promise, the manipulation of the carnivalesque, and, above all, the self-satisfied, smugly ironic, and strangely affectionate relationship between duper and duped, trickster and tricked, advertiser and audience. If American culture has lacked for royalty, it is not for want of a real Prince of Humbug.

LYDIA E. PINKHAM'S VEGETABLE COMPOUND

Personalizing the Corporate Face

IN THE 1920s a famous literary critic at Oxford University played a whimsical but profound trick on his graduate students. He gave them a sheaf of miscellaneous poems—some written by "great masters," some written by also-rans, some even written by himself— and asked them to evaluate them as "works of art." If great art is self-evident, he thought, then surely these future teachers will be able to distinguish creative genius from popular dross.

They couldn't do it. They were just as likely to mistake the treacle of a Hallmark card for the masterful confection of an Elizabethan sonnet. Why?

Because creativity is not as simple as it seems. Often it does not knock your socks off, and sometimes it changes how you put your socks on. Lasting creativity makes subtle connections that not only stand the test of time, but actually change the way we experience events. What Shakespeare did first, Hallmark is still doing. If you don't know the dates and titles, it's often hard to know which came first. Worse still, if you don't know precise authorship, it's sometimes hard to tell quality. That's why the debate over who really wrote some of Shakespeare's works—was it Francis Bacon, Christopher Marlowe, the Earl of Oxford, even Queen Elizabeth —still rages. That's why modern painters sign their paintings.

Have a look at American patent medicine ads around the turn of the twentieth century if you want to see how complicated it is to separate wheat from chaff. "Patent" medicine is really a misnomer with American products, since the *patent* really refers to an agreement with the Crown to license (and tax) an English

"Her face, her face, they publish her face": Lydia Pinkham newspaper cut, 1880s.

product. But then again, "medicine" is hardly the right word either, as most of these products were about 20 percent alcohol or, better yet, a tincture of opium or cocaine.

Oddly enough, the Civil War had created thousands of eager consumers for what was generally known as "the soldier's disease." In 1870, Americans consumed half a million pounds of opium and its morphine derivative, mostly by way of patent medicines. For the first time in American culture, the concept of killing pain had become a reality, and industries were sprouting up to fill this new need. "Grin and bear it" had become "Drink this."

No matter what such remedies were called, these new brewed-in-the-kitchen industries depended on cutting-edge advertising for their tonics. After all, since what was added to the depressant was water and miscellaneous gunk, it didn't matter much what you called it. Just consider some of these names: Swamproot Compound, Kickapoo Sagwa, Pitcher's Castoria, Warner's Kidney Cure, Hadacol, Katonka, Snake Oil, Dr. Moog's Love Balm, Spanish Fly, and various Universal Balms. They all promised the same swig of painkiller.

As well, since the package was almost always a glass bottle, the container really wasn't important. It was what you put on the label and in the advertising that really moved the stuff off the shelves.

Human anatomy in a bottle: *Dr. Kilmer and Company Standard Herbal Remedies, 1885.*

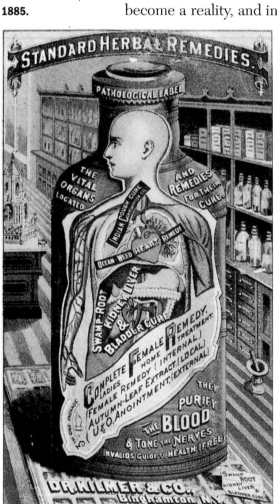

"Bells and whistles" barely describes the outrageously creative copy and pupil-dilating art of patent-medicine advertising. Some of the most sublime commercial artwork ever produced was lavished on picturing the restorative results of these pick-me-ups. We have lost many of these images because the medium in which they appeared most often has simply disappeared.

That medium was the trade card, a little rectangle of 40-weight paper that could hold the inks of a new printing process, lithography. On one side of the card was an attention-getting image. On the other side—the "verso"—was the message, the pitch. Just as television is today misnomered "free," so the trade card was given away, free. You paid for it not in coin but in time spent reading the verso, the advertisement.

In the eighteenth century the trade card did just what it claimed: on one side an engraved image, on the other the name of your trade, your business—just like the modern business card. But by the mid-eighteenth century a new process of printing had been developed, using specially prepared blocks of limestone and grease crayons, which vastly expanded the artistic possibilities. Now the engraver could draw rather than carve out his images. But what revolutionized lithography and transformed the trade card was the first application of colored inks.

Chromolithography allowed the mass production of images using different colors from differently inked printing stones. In the place of a few artfully engraved lines was a starburst of free-hand imagery and colorful excitement.

Trade cards were produced by the thousands. Once the lithographic "stones" were replaced by zinc plates, and steam power was applied to the presses, trade cards were all over the country. Because newsprint was so expensive and because magazines and newspapers were still hesitant to sell their space to any commercial interest (let alone to any company of questionable pedigree), companies with newly branded products started using the cards as hand-to-hand advertising.

The cards were distributed by drummers who carried packages of the cards along with the products. The cards would be there on the counter of your local general store, free for the taking. The major collectors of this "paper ephemera" were children, who, as brewers and cigarette makers today will tell you, are just the right age to be introduced to the effects of alcohol and drugs.

Later the cards were stuck in the packaging of products as part of a series to be collected. Many of the early brands of cigarettes were started because the young smokers cared more about collecting cards—called "stiffeners," as they held the package upright—than favoring a particular taste. The cards featuring buxom burlesque queens were so popular that they spun off to become "bachelor" cards, which one had to purchase, as well as small calendar cards, a vestige of which can still be seen on garage walls today as the "girlie calendar." Still later, decorated trade cards were mailed to customers as a way of saying thanks. From this came the modern tradition of sending Christmas cards, a rare example of a commercial practice coopted by individual use.

The patent medicine companies, among the first to see the potential of trade cards, used them better, more creatively, and to greater advantage than anyone else. Their cards were works of high lithographic art, more often than not picturing the results of using their product. Because creating scenes of utopian good health can be so colorful, and because there were so many competitors producing essentially the same brew, the advertising had to be eye-catching. Not only were patent-medicine trade cards glorious, they were uniformly over the top. In patent medicine ads we see the most amazing transformations ever wrought by the human imagination on the human condition. Old wheezers breathe easy, blocked digestive tracts become superhighways, and potency—always potency—is restored to levels a goat would be proud of.

The verso text could often be as outrageous as the beckoning lithographed image. In fact, the flip side of the trade card is the beginning of a primary tradition in the advertising business: if you can't make it better, make it up. Here, for instance, is the boiler-plate claim of Lydia E. Pinkham's Vegetable Compound on the trade cards of the 1880s:

> It will cure entirely the worst form of Female Complaints, all Ovar-ian troubles, Inflammation, Ulceration, Falling and Displacements of the Womb and the consequent Spinal Weakness, and is par-ticularly adapted to the Change of Life. It removes faintness, flat-ulency, destroys all craving for stimulants, and relieves weakness of the stomach. It cures Bloating, Headaches, Nervous Prostra-tion, General Debility, Sleeplessness, Depression and Indigestion.

After reading this claim, one can understand why the phrase "ethical drug manufacturers" took hold in the 1920s. Little won-der that the scientific industry wanted to differentiate itself from the patent-medicine charlatans. But before you dismiss the entire category as bogus, consider that most of the prestigious pharma-ceutical houses of today were constructed over the backyard sheds of patent medicine: Eli Lilly became an apprentice at the Good Samaritan Drug Store selling kickapoo juice; Henry Wellcome went to work for McKesson & Robbins selling "compressed med-icines"; Lunsford Richardson sold his Croup and Pneumonia Salve in North Carolina. Their namesake companies (Lilly, Bur-roughs Wellcome, Richardson-Vicks) are now at the forefront of better living through chemistry.

By the 1880s the panacea industry was spending almost 40 percent of its gross on advertising, producing more than half the trade cards in circulation. Remember, since the medicines were indistinguishable, the cards *had* to innovate. Like the blue jeans advertisers today, little was lost by being outrageous.

This ad for Lydia Pinkham's Vegetable Compound was probably the most successful of its kind. It appeared as a trade card, as a newspaper ad, and as the product label. While the product was a concoction of unicorn root, black cohosh, and fenugreek seed (along with the requisite booze to "keep the product from freezing"), this image was pure gold. It was used on trade cards of the 1880s and in the newsprint of the 1940s, and sold a lot of product.

When this image was pulled from circulation in the financial panic of the 1890s, sales tumbled by nearly 80 percent. When it was returned to circulation over the next decade, annual sales increased almost 2,500 percent! One might say that the second-greatest creative activity surrounding this image was that the content was left pretty much untouched.

The tonic itself was only modified five times, and only then to keep the feds and Carry Nation at bay. The original concoction was first brewed in 1843 by a young schoolteacher in Lynn, Massachusetts, Lydia Estes. Once she married Isaac Pinkham, she resigned her teaching position, which was a bad mistake. He was a business failure in everything but ballyhooing his wife's vegetable-based remedy.

Lydia assumed responsibility for the formula, modified it somewhat in her kitchen, and dispensed it periodically, without fee, to family and neighbors. Word of mouth was so strong that groups of women would make the trek out from Boston. Its commercial promise was not realized for years, but when Lydia E. Pinkham's Vegetable Compound was finally marketed (now fully fortified with 18 percent alcohol), its sales brought it to the fore-front of patent medicines.

Why did this concoction not just survive but prevail? The genius was not Lydia or Isaac, but their son Dan. Although his name is rarely acknowledged in the pantheon of advertising geniuses, it should be. Here's some of what he did. Once he paid young women to write on small cards, "Try Lydia E. Pinkham's Vegetable Compound and I know it will cure you, it's the best

THE GREAT EAST RIVER SUSPENSION BRIDGE.
CONNECTING THE CITIES OF NEW YORK & BROOKLYN.
The Bridge crosses the river in a single span of 1595 ft. suspended by four cables 15½ inches in diameter.   The approach on the New York side is 2492 ft. the approach on the Brooklyn side is 1901 ft. Total length 5988 ft. From high water to roadway 120 ft. From roadway to top 157 ft. From high water to centre of span 135 ft. Width of bridge 85 ft. Total height of Towers 277 ft.

thing for Uterine complaints there is. From your cousin, Mary— P.S. You can get it at…" He then scattered the cards around cemeteries on the days before Decoration Day. He also printed a trade card with a realistic engraving of the Brooklyn Bridge, the greatest engineering marvel of the age. Under the main span hung what must have been the largest banner of all times: Lydia E. Pinkham's Vegetable Compound. That such a sign existed only on the trade card mattered not at all. What mattered was that mil-

The powers of mythical association: Lydia Pinkham trade card, 1880s.

lions of Americans were fully convinced that the sign was there. He conned small-town newspapers into carrying favorable news stories, and even editorial endorsements of the tonic, in exchange for generous advertising contracts.

Dan experimented with fold-in newspaper inserts, trial-size bottles, and even product placement. He encouraged Lydia Pinkham jokes and songs—anything to get his mother's name into common usage and branded into common consciousness. Although other companies had used personal testimony from satisfied users in advertising copy, Dan put these comments in small print under the bold headline that the company would pay five thousand dollars to anyone who could prove the testimony was not unsolicited. Thus he gave people a reason to read the fine print.

If imitation is the sincerest form of flattery, then consider that in one ad Mrs. Pinkham urges women to "reach for a vegetable instead of a sweet." A generation later the headline was appropriated by Lucky Strike cigarettes and refashioned into "Reach for a Lucky Instead of a Sweet."

The genius to target "weak women" was Dan's, and he kept his eye on the target until he experienced a nervous breakdown of his own. His marketing plan was the essence of simplicity. Find a niche audience, in this case the thousands of farm wives who then toiled from dawn to dusk, who looked old before their time, and who had every reason to feel tuckered out. Build a relationship between them and the image of his mother. "Keep Everlastingly at It," as the early slogan for the N. W. Ayer & Son agency put it. Put Lydia's picture everywhere—on trade cards, on billboards, in newspapers, on barns. Change the product if you must, but never change the advertising.

Dan knew the secret of the placebo: you ingest the hype, not the drug. The advertising makes you feel better.

In the print ad, on the trade card, and on the bottle's label, Lydia always presents herself only in outline. We never see her fleshed in. That outline captures all the archetypal power of the grandmother-as-sage. There is no personality to speak of here, only the confident sternness of someone who's been there, done that. Atop her prim Quaker frock, she looks out at us without blinking. No funny business, she says, this is serious. You are sick. I know what's best.

And what she knows is this: If you are a woman, you cannot trust doctors to understand your plight. She says as much in the laurel surrounding her face: WOMAN CAN SYMPATHIZE WITH WOMAN. HEALTH OF WOMAN IS THE HOPE OF THE RACE. This is not a criticism of male medicine as much as a simple reiteration of female truth. Men just don't get it. That's all there is to it. If women know what girls must learn, then grannies know it best.

Note, however, that halfway through the copy, men are let in for a little surcease. Not only does this stuff work for "generative organs of either sex," but "KIDNEY COMPLAINTS of Either Sex Find Great Relief in Its Use." Has there ever been a better segue from a "have to have" to a "nice to have" audience? Little wonder that "Physicians use it and prescribe it fully," even though you may be assured they don't understand how it works. What do they know of Female Weaknesses? Have their wombs ever fallen?

No image today, not the swoosh, the golden arches, or even the Coke can, can rival the visage of Lydia two generations ago. The product is not the hero, she is. She is as confident as she is caring. She writes "Yours in health" and she boldly signs her name. In fact, you could write to her and your letter would never be seen by a man, never, ever. She "freely answers all letters" and, in true direct-marketing style, asks only that you *mention this paper*. (Even today, the privacy of what must be one of the largest collections of genuine female concern is not available for scholars.) A woman would respond to your letter and it would be signed by Lydia (long after she was no more). Talk about relationship marketing!

However, better than the promise of confidentiality was the lack of copyright. Lydia's image was not registered. It was allowed to travel freely, which it did—and then some. In a world that had few shared engraved "cuts"—aside from the Sunday-school Bible renditions of Christ—Lydia rivaled Queen Victoria as the most recognized woman of her day. After all, her image was in the compositing bins of almost every newspaper in the land. So, when a printer wanted an appropriate illustration, he simply removed Lydia's verbal garland and placed her outline atop his story.

One of the most popular collegiate drinking songs of the day was "The Lydia Pinkham Song." After a number of verses, the most famous of which is

> *Widow Brown she had no children,*
> *Though she loved them very dear;*
> *So she took some Vegetable Compound,*
> *Now she has them twice a year!*

comes the refrain:

> *OO-H-H, we'll sing of Lydia Pinkham,*
> *And her love for the Human Race,*
> *How she sells her Vegetable Compound,*
> *And the papers, the papers they publish,*
>   *they publish her FACE!*

If one had to isolate the creative insight behind Lydia Pinkham's presentation, it is that we hear the corporate voice and recognize it as trustworthy. Cutting through the chatter of innumerable "feel better fast" spiels, comes her heartfelt concern for a woman's health. Long before we learned to talk about corporations as personalities, the persona of Lydia was doing the heavy lifting. She cares.

Thanks to Lydia, corporations have never stopped talking. Sometimes they speak from the mouths of real people. Think of Lee Iacocca, Frank Perdue, or Leona Helmsley. The problem is that often age, retirement, or bad press removes the spokesperson. So sometimes corporations hire a mouthpiece, as with Robert Young for Nescafé, James Garner for Polaroid, or Michael Jordan for Nike. The problem here is that sometimes they go AWOL. Remember O.J. Simpson for Hertz. So it's clearly best to have a corporate icon who can both speak and behave. Here we find our good friends Ronald McDonald, Betty Crocker, Miss Clairol, Mr. Clean, and all their mythic brethren—eternally neat, clean, and well-behaved. Certainly the grandmother of them all—the real people, the paid people, and the pretend people is the redoubtable Lydia Pinkham. Next to her, the Marlboro Man seems like a bewildered cowpoke.

PEARS' SOAP

John E. Millais's *A Child's World* and the Powers of Associated Value

3

THE GREAT INTELLECTUAL ENDEAVOR of Victorian education was to divide and conquer. What was to be divided was culture, and it was to be divided into high and low, good-for-you and bad-for-you. What was to be conquered was the rising tide of mobocracy that carried vulgarity into every corner of human culture. Thanks to the steam-powered printing press, the mob now had its own culture, its own images, and was becoming too powerful to be contained. The very word "mob," a Victorian coinage, carried the threat to established standards within its etymology. "Mob" was short for *mobile vulgus*: the rabble on the move.

As well, not by happenstance was "consumption" the term used to describe both tuberculosis and the result of a new plague, commercialism, the application of advertised value to machine-made things. These people, the mobs, were consuming things—all the wrong things!

The institution that was to do the dividing and conquering was education—*compulsory* education. It was in school that the differences between pulp novels and literature were taught; in school that you learned that classical music was better than dance-hall music; and there, as well, that you learned "art appreciation." You were introduced to "the best that had been thought and said," not just because it was intrinsically better, but because knowing it allowed you to separate yourself from the unruly, the unwashed, the mob.

The reason this separation was so important was that the machine age was rapidly making everyone equal, at least in the marketplace. So a body of material—the canon—was separated

Thomas J. Barratt's adaptation of John E. Millais's *Bubbles* for Pears' soap, 1888.

PEARS' SOAP
A SPECIALTY FOR IMPROVING THE COMPLEXION
AND PREVENTING REDNESS ROUGHNES
AND CHAPPING RECOMMENDED
BY MRS. LANGTRY, MADAME PATTI &c
AND OBTAINED
15 INTERNATIONAL MEDALS
AS A COMPLEXION SOAP.
PEARS

out and made the special province of the educated elite. One experienced the canon in newly created tabernacles: the museum, the symphony hall, and the university.

Because the canon was gathering accepted value, it was ripe for the picking. What a delicious irony for the advertiser. If you could associate your mass-produced, and hence vulgar, product with other objects in the privileged category of "art," you were heads above the competition. The difference between trash and antique is often only in their placement. Again, the words betray the hidden structure. After all, what were *objets d'art* but objects thought valuable enough to paint? Only later did the word come to mean the objects themselves. Put your dandelion in with a bouquet of roses and it soon becomes a yellow rose.

In advertising jargon, this is called "associated value" and it is the reason why, if you want to sell a Buick, you picture it outside an exclusive golf club, why T-shirts are heavy with polo ponies, and why caviar costs more than mere fish eggs. When you want to borrow value for an object, you insert it near objects of established value. Proximity implies similarity. Value leaks.

At about the same time that P. T. Barnum was discovering the power of hype, the principle of association was being exploited by one of the grandest figures in advertising history, Thomas J. Barratt. While Barnum learned about advertising by selling the exotic, Barratt learned by selling the mundane. He learned how to generate value for one of the most undifferentiated products of the machine age—soap.

The manufacture of soap is a turning point in civilization. Old-style soap, made on the farm, was the result of boiling animal fats and wood ashes. It was molded into balls and, after a while, it started to stink. New-style soap, made by machines, was a combination of caustic soda and vegetable fats. It was pressed into bars and it lasted forever.

However, it was hard to differentiate among machine-made soaps. They were all the same. In 1881, a plant employee working for James Gamble in Cincinnati, Ohio, left the aerating machinery running too long and produced a batch of soap that was lighter than water. It floated. Gamble claimed that it floated because it was pure; in fact, we all know how pure: $99^{44}/_{100}$ percent pure. Associating your soap with purity was one way to sell soap.

In England, Andrew Pears had developed another most peculiar soap. The soap was translucent and hence seemingly already "clean." Pears positioned his soap to appeal to the English upper class's desire to lighten their skin color, and hence separate themselves from those who toiled out in the sun. The mob didn't use this soap. Problem was, then as now, you couldn't *say* that; it was not politically correct to the Victorians who invented the term *mob*. You could come close, as did Pond's Vanishing Cream, which touted itself as "softens and whitens the skin." The trick would be to associate the soap with an upper-class product, something already certified as pure, so you wouldn't have to say anything. It would be understood.

Pears's son-in-law, Thomas J. Barratt, would make the connection between being clean and feeling clean. Before hitting on art (literally!) as a way to resolve his problem, Barratt had some other creative ideas. For instance, he purchased a quarter of a million French ten-centime pieces (accepted in lieu of English pennies) and had "Pears'" stamped on each of them. Although there was a law against defacing domestic currency, no such law governed foreign coins so he simply put the coins into circulation.

Like modern companies that attempt to make their slogans part of daily language—like "Just Do It," "You Deserve a Break Today," or even "Where's the Beef?"—Barratt painted "Good Morning! Have You Used Your Pears' Soap?" on blank spaces all over the British Empire. He also attempted to insert the question into the national census form that was sent to every household in the country. No soap, said the British government. Still, he succeeded to such an extent that it was said that genteel people were bashful about greeting each other with the "good morning" salutation, lest they be contaminated with his advertising lingo.

He also started the dubious tradition of bombarding new parents with trial-size baby products. If mention of your baby's birth appeared in *The Times*, you would soon be receiving a cake of soap and a handful of leaflets on baby care.

Barratt began to understand the power of association after he cajoled doctors and professors to testify to Pears' purity. He even persuaded the influential American preacher Henry Ward Beecher to equate godliness and cleanliness and Pears' soap. Endorsement in hand, he bought the entire front page of the *New York Herald* to display the endorsement. Sales rocketed.

As Barratt was learning, although endorsement depends on association, such testimony doesn't have to make literal sense; all it has to do is link spokesperson and product in an *emotional* way. That's why Michael Jordan, who we usually see covered in a fine glow of sweat, can successfully sell his own cologne. Logic would suggest he should sell an antiperspirant. Barratt's most powerful endorsement for Pears' came from a famous beauty, the actress Lillie Langtry. She declared, "I have much pleasure in stating that I have used your soap for some time and prefer it to any other." Barratt saw to it that everyone in the civilized world heard what she had to say. He did not have to mention what really activated Ms. Langtry's words: she was best known as King Edward VII's mistress. In a sense, she was dirty. But in a contrary sense she was not as good as royalty, she was better. She was what royalty *wanted*.

Barratt knew that when association works, the common product is made part of an elevated network of things. Champagne is no longer perceived as a wine, it is a drink for those who also consume, say, expensive jewelry, elegant clothes, and art.

Getting Pears' soap *into* a certified work of art was Barratt's creative coup d'advertising. Here he was successful beyond even his inflated expectations. Barratt made high culture, the very culture that abominated advertising, do his work for him.

In the 1880s, John Everett Millais was the most popular and famous painter in England. In upper-crust circles he was well known for being a founding member of that raffish set, the Pre-Raphaelite Brotherhood. Among commoners he was known as the Great Artist, knighted for his contribution to high culture, and president of the Royal Academy.

Since he was not "to the manor born," Millais had to sell his paintings, and indeed he did. One of them, a portrait of his cherubic grandson (the future Admiral Sir William James) called *A Child's World,* he sold to Sir William Ingram of the *Illustrated London News.* Ingram, as he was legally entitled to do, used the image as a full-page illustration in the 1887 Christmas issue.

Like other magazines of the time, the *ILN* was engaged in the circulation-building endeavor of covering its pages with "images suitable for framing." Rather like "sweeps week," in which the television networks put out their best product in order to garner the highest Nielsen ratings, Victorian magazines used the Christmas season to boost circulation and showcase their printing expertise. The Victorian reading public, now educated to the importance of displaying good taste, framed these inserts, and hung them around the house. Parlors started to resemble museums because art was becoming a sign of having good taste.

These elaborate chromolithographs, shortened to "chromos," demonstrated that such state-of-the-art printing could sustain entire industries. On one hand, these inserts sprung loose to become an industry we still recognize, the mass-produced poster. On the other, photolithography made the process so cheap that a new genre was born—the modern picture magazine like *Life* or *Look.* Advertising went along for the ride, paying the freight.

A Child's World, soon retitled *Bubbles,* gained a vast following, thanks to the massive print run of the *ILN* and the poster that
followed. The scene was an apt image of the times, for it portrayed
the maudlin sentimentality of childhood so popular with aspiring
middle-class Victorians. Children were not seen as incomplete
adults, as the eighteenth century had portrayed them, but as
incomplete angels. Look at what was happening to Victorian children's clothing and you can see the results of this transformation.
The outfit that young William James has on, his bee-stung lips, his
halo of curls, and his upturned eyes are all part of a pattern. All he
lacks are wings.

Since the Child is Father of the Man and "a darling of a pygmy
size," as Wordsworth said; since the noble savage was the ideal, as
Rousseau said; since the preadolescent was "divine philosopher,"
as Coleridge said; then what better icon of soap-cleaned innocence? And what more apt an image of transitory perfection of
childhood than that perfect little bubble of soap? We need not see
it go pop; that will happen soon enough.

This connection between children = innocence, innocence =
cleanliness, and cleanliness = Pears' soap was to become one of
the greatest advertising campaigns ever. Ingram, the publisher,
thinking he had "used up" the value of *Bubbles,* sold it to Barratt,
the advertiser. As opposed to our culture, in which repetition
often increases the value of the unique painting (the French
Impressionists, for example, sell for inflated prices because they
are well known around the world), a few generations ago it was
thought that machine duplication lessened value. If everyone had
a chromo of the *Mona Lisa,* then the original was thought to be
compromised.

What really "ruined" this unique painting, however, was not
just that it was wrenched from high culture and inducted into the
system of commodities, but that Barratt had the audacity to have
Pears engraved on the cake of soap in the picture's lower fore-

ground. He took a proof sheet of what he had done to the painter's studio and made this pitch to Millais: If you think art is important and if you want everyone to benefit from viewing it, then give me your permission to reprint your painting with just this little visual addition. I'll distribute it free to thousands of budding art lovers all over the globe. It will foster art appreciation. Millais bit. In a few years Barratt had spent more than $6 million—a staggering sum, especially then—saturating the British Empire with an image he had purchased for thousands.

Little did Millais know at the time, but the transaction blurred, for the first time and forevermore, the bright line between art and advertising, between high culture and the vulgar, between pristine and corrupt. For years the debate would flare up in the letters to *The Times*.

Marie Corelli, a popular novelist of the day, straightaway put these words in the mouth of a character in her book *The Sorrows of Satan*:

> I am one of those who think the fame of Millais as an artist was marred when he degraded himself to the level of painting the little green boy blowing bubbles of Pears' soap. *That was an advertisement,* and that very incident in his career, trifling as it seems, will prevent his ever standing on the dignified height of distinction with such masters in Art as Romney, Sir Peter Lely, Gainsborough and Reynolds [in Turner 1953, 153].

Although Millais was able to persuade Mrs. Corelli to remove this offhand comment in future editions, it was too late. The die was cast.

Barratt couldn't have cared less. He had once said that any fool could make soap, but that it took a clever man to sell it, and he had been proven correct. Pears "owned" the concept of art, literally.

Although Barratt may have singlemindedly sought to exploit what Victorians were so busily rending asunder, namely art and commerce, his descendants still carry the torch. Most of his disciples are in the advertising world. Witness, for example, the never-ending use of the word *art* in such slogans as Louis Vuitton luggage ("the art of travel"), *Gourmet* magazine ("the art of good eating"), Martell Cognac ("L'art de M*artell*"), Credit Suisse ("the art of Swiss banking"), Sony portable phones ("the art of conversation"), Tiffany's ("the art of shopping"), Cartier ("the art of being unique"), the Sub-Zero refrigerator ("the art of refrigeration"), Air France ("the art of flying"), the Caribbean Island of St. Barts ("discover the art of gracious living"), Mont Blanc pens ("the art of writing")....

And this is to say nothing of the wholesale lifting of high-culture imagery and setting it down next to images of fast-selling consumer goods. We share a common knowledge of such works as the *Mona Lisa*, Michelangelo's *David*, Botticelli's *Primavera*, Munch's *The Scream*, Van Gogh's landscapes, Matisse's cutouts, Mondrian's squares, Magritte's juxtapositions, Seurat's *Sunday Afternoon on the Island of La Grande Jatte*, Leutze's *George Washington Crossing the Delaware*, Wood's *American Gothic*, Whistler's *Portrait of the Artist's Mother*, or Henri Rousseau's sad-eyed jungle cats, not from Art History 101, but from seeing them in advertisements for what? Beer, cheese, booze, cigarettes.

One can "hear" the same phenomenon with certain strains of once-classical music. For instance, advertising has captured the finale to Rossini's "*William Tell* Overture," the "Summer" section of Vivaldi's *The Four Seasons*, the Second Movement of Beethoven's *Symphony No. 9*, Shostakovich's "The Gadfly," Strauss's "Blue Danube," Gounod's "Funeral March of a Marionette," or Smetana's "Dance of the Comedians."

More ironically, Barratt's real progeny are now in high culture. While painters like Dalí, Toulouse-Lautrec, and Picasso may have incorporated commercial images into their works, by the 1950s the works of certain artists often *became* commercial images. What was it that the Pop artists had in mind if not to celebrate the connection between art and commerce? Pop art was simply that: *popular* art, art that made no pretense about distinctions, art that joyfully collapsed hierarchies, art that celebrated what we share, and, most annoyingly for those who cherish the myth of the alienated artist, art dedicated to making money. "To me," said Andy Warhol, sounding rather like Thomas J. Barratt, "business is the highest form of art."

In a way, Pop art repaid the tribute of *Bubbles.* If art gave associational value to commercialism, then commercialism could lend a hand to art. If Barratt made art into kitsch, Pop could make kitsch into art. What were the subjects of Pop? Ballantine beer cans, Brillo soap pad boxes, Campbell's Soup cans, Spaghetti-Os, VWs, Mott's apple juice, Kellogg's Corn Flakes, Del Monte peach halves, Lipton soup mixes, Lucky Strikes, Coca-Cola bottles, huge hamburgers and lipsticks ... you name it, if it had life near the soap aisle, it was captured in Pop. Turnabout is fair play. What goes around, comes around.

In a sense Barratt has been, if not vindicated, then at least acknowledged. He knew what Renaissance artisans and patrons had first learned long ago: The hand that holds the money is often more powerful than the hand that grasps the palette. When Michelangelo's *Creation of Adam* appears in publicity campaigns for ties, hotels, stereos, and banks, we are apt to decry the sacrilege. We forget that the Sistine Chapel was painted to order, on receipt of a chit from the Pope, as a biblical advertisement. Talk about the powers of association!

PEPSODENT

Claude Hopkins and the Magic of the Preemptive Claim

4

WHAT DICKENS WAS to the traditional novel, what Picasso was to modern art, what Elvis was to rock 'n' roll, Claude Hopkins was to advertising. He inherited a form, a mode of expression, and he forever transformed it. He did this not because he wanted fame and riches, but because he passionately loved the endeavor. As Dickens was born to write, Picasso to paint, Elvis to sing, Hopkins was here on earth to sell.

Like his brethren, he started early. According to his delightfully self-serving *My Life in Advertising* (1923), Hopkins seems to have spent his formative years happily going from house to house distributing flyers, reselling books, and marketing his mother's silver polish. He exuded gusto. Yet, as David Ogilvy would later recall of his own door-to-door selling, there is no better introduction to advertising than attempting to cross the threshold of a stranger's door and get into the parlor. No one made as many trips across that threshold as did young Claude Hopkins, and no one spent as much time in the parlor.

And certainly no one was as scientific about it. Hopkins's other book is titled *Scientific Advertising* (1927). What distinguishes this version of his life's work is that we observe Hopkins observing himself in a strangely detached way, a kind of Heisenberg explanation of himself selling. His experiences are coming to us from a detached, almost omniscient, observer. He continually refers to himself in the third person, almost as if he were as curious as Darwin following some four-toed finch. Hopkins clearly wants it this way, for his whole point is that "advertising is based on fixed

Magic
Lies in pretty teeth—Remove that film

Why will any woman in these days have dingy film on teeth?

There is now a way to end it. Millions of people employ it. You can see the results in glistening teeth everywhere you look.

This is to offer a ten-day test, to show *you* how to beautify the teeth.

Film is cloudy

Film is that viscous coat you feel. It clings to the teeth, enters crevices and stays. When left it forms the basis of tartar. Teeth look discolored more or less.

But film does more. It causes most tooth troubles.

It holds food substances which ferment and form acid. It holds the acid in contact with the teeth to cause decay. Germs breed by millions in it. They, with tartar, are the chief cause of pyorrhea.

Avoid Harmful Grit

Pepsodent curdles the film and removes it without harmful scouring. Its polishing agent is far softer than enamel. Never use a film combatant which contains harsh grit.

You leave it

Old ways of brushing leave much of that film intact. It dims the teeth and, night and day, threatens serious damage. That's why so many well-brushed teeth discolor and decay. Tooth troubles have been constantly increasing. So dental science has been seeking ways to fight that film.

A new-type tooth paste has been perfected, correcting some old mistakes. These two film combatants are embodied in it. The name is Pepsodent, and by its use millions now combat that film.

Two other foes

It also fights two other foes of teeth. It multiplies the starch digestant in the saliva. To digest starch deposits on teeth which may otherwise cling and form acids.

It multiplies the alkalinity of the saliva. To neutralize mouth acids which cause tooth decay.

Lives altered

Whole lives may be altered by this better tooth protection. Dentists now advise that children use Pepsodent from the time the first tooth appears. It will mean a new dental era.

The way to know this is to send the coupon for a 10-Day Tube. Note how clean the teeth feel after using. Mark the absence of the viscous film. See how teeth whiten as the film-coats disappear.

See and feel the new effects, then read the reasons in the book we send.

Cut out the coupon now.

Pepsodent
PAT. OFF.
REG. U.S.

The New-Day Dentifrice

A scientific film combatant, which whitens, cleans and protects the teeth without the use of harmful grit. Now advised by leading dentists the world over.

---

principles and done according to fundamental laws." Would that it were so.

While Hopkins may take physics and chemistry as the scientific templates of selling, biology might be better. Members of the same species generally behave alike. So should a species of advertisment, once defined and classified accurately. Of course, even members of the same species behave differently in different circumstances. So, inevitably, will ads—no matter how similar. And that is as close as selling will ever come to being a science. As one wag has suggested, the science advertising most resembles is farming. You scatter the seed, come back in a few months, and harvest the crop. Sometimes there is no crop.

But no matter. Hopkins's thesis is that one must accept human desires, and never try to change them. The goal of the advertiser is to get in the path of desire—what today is called "positioning." Before Hopkins, advertisers depended on their own intuition. In fact, they often insisted on it. After Hopkins came the rise of research, the rise of analytical psychology, the rise of taking the audience seriously.

Hopkins gets in the way of human desire by establishing a *reason why* the object for sale needs your consideration. Sounds simple, but it isn't. The key is that the *reason why* often has little to do with the product. In fact, often it is a characteristic shared by all other products in the same category. So, to be precise, what Hopkins developed is better called a "preemptive" *reason why*.

Here's how it works. When Hopkins was selling the Bissell carpet sweeper, he never discussed how well it worked, but rather the colorful wooden finishes and the fact that it would make a nifty Christmas present. In fact, he called it "The Queen of Christmas Presents!" When selling Swift & Company's Cotosuet shortening, he never talked about the qualities of this lard, but about the restaurants that used the product. Selling Schlitz beer, he never cited the brew, only that the bottles were "washed with live steam!" When he advertised VanCamp's pork and beans, he stressed that the beans were baked for hours at 245 degrees. He said that Goodyear tires were for "all weather." To him, Palmolive soap was a beauty bar (used by Cleopatra!), not a cleanser. And, most famously, when working for Quaker Oats, he changed the name Wheat Berries to Puffed Wheat and sold it along with Puffed Rice as foods amazingly "shot from guns," "grains puffed to eight times normal size," and "125 million steam explosions caused in every kernel."

In each case you can see how Hopkins is crossing the threshold on his way into your parlor. He never compares his product with a competitor. He never mentions price. He never makes a joke, even though he is sometimes at the edge of the ridiculous. What he is doing is claiming some aspect of the product that is *not* unique, and then attempting to "own" this aspect. What the audience may know, but does not question, is that the proffered *reason why* obtains to all competitors. Other carpet sweepers had wood trim; other restaurants used lard in baking; all beer brewers steam cleaned bottles; every can of canned beans had to be cooked at 245 degrees; all soap beautified, and all puffed-grain cereals were heated until the kernels popped.

In generating these preemptive claims, Hopkins is unfolding the central insight in selling modern interchangeable goods. After all, the Industrial Revolution was the application of machinery to production, and that meant that your machine makes almost the same product as does my machine. Hopkins explains how to sell what are now called "fast-moving consumer goods" (FMCGs):

> We tell simple facts, common to all makers in the line—too common to be told because the article is not unique. It embodies no

great advantages. Perhaps countless people can make similar products. But tell the pains you take to excel. Tell factors and features which others deem too commonplace to claim. Your product will come to typify those excellencies. If others claim them afterward, it will only serve to advertise you [Hopkins 1991, 84–85].

What you are doing as an advertiser is preempting the equal claims of others by omitting the obvious. In so doing, you are staking a claim not just around the product, but in the mind of your audience. When the advertising for Lucky Strike cigarettes said, "It's toasted," it did not mention that all tobacco was flue-cured. When Tetley Tea said they had "tiny little tea leaves," they neglected to say their leaves were the same size as their competitors'. Ditto Wonder Bread "helping build strong bodies twelve ways." Or, more recently, when Extra-Strength Tylenol exhorts, "You can't buy a more potent pain reliever without a prescription," you are not informed that other analgesics also contain the maximum nonprescription levels of painkiller.

In modern branding, this colonizing of consciousness extends past product interchangeability into the realm of complex associations. Think only of how Pepsi links itself to the concept of the new generation, how the night belongs to Michelob (giving up after-work drinking to Miller time), how Kodak owns special moments, how Merrill Lynch's bull asserts confidence in the market, how Marlboro stakes a claim to the West, how Ford is Quality and Chevrolet is Americana, how Virginia Slims co-opts the women's movement while Nike controls basketball, and, well, you know the rest.

The central truth in the preemptive claim is that the advertiser must never tell a howler. Just as nothing hastens the demise of a bad product quicker than good advertising, nothing is more dangerous to a good product than an outright lie. There *is* truth in advertising, a very special kind of truth.

Hopkins found which truth to claim by carefully tagging all variant advertisements with a coupon. The claim that was most effective was the claim that elicited the most coupons. In this sense, Hopkins really was scientific. He realized that you could not predict the workings of human desire, but you could follow it with split-run tests, sampling technology, and direct-response canvassing. Never offer discounts. Never raise your voice. Always make the customer initiate the transaction. His favorite quote was that no argument in the world can possibly compare to one dramatic demonstration. Such a demonstration makes the customer open the door and invite you in.

That innocuous little coupon is powder on the customer's tail. You follow it back to the nest and you find where the flock is heading. Or, in Hopkins's own atavistic analogy:

> People are like sheep. They cannot judge values, nor can you and I. We judge things largely by others' impressions, by popular favor. We go with the crowd. So the most effective thing I have ever found in advertising is the trend of the crowd [Hopkins 1991, 119].

So here, in the 1920s, was Pepsodent toothpaste. Good name, interchangeable product, bad advertising. The company was going bankrupt, and, as was often the case, Hopkins took an equity position rather than a salary. What he did to Pepsodent in four years would make him a millionaire. It would make Pepsodent the best-selling toothpaste until the 1950s.

Hopkins knew that the logical way to sell toothpaste was to claim that it prevents decay. But he also knew that assertion was a baldfaced lie. Pepsodent was just like all its competitors—the same abrasives, suspended in a gel, packed in a tube. Hopkins remembers,

> When I urged any person to buy Pepsodent, I was met with apathy. When I asked them to send ten cents for a sample, they almost ignored me. So I was forced to altruistic advertising. The sample was free for the good of the parties concerned. I never even mentioned that Pepsodent was for sale. I never quoted the price [Hopkins 1991, 119].

Forget moving them to the toothpaste, just move them to the coupon. He still had to get them to open the door, however, before he could get into the parlor.

Hopkins did this by asserting the glaringly obvious and, in so doing, removed it from the assertions of others. Rubbing almost anything soft on the teeth gives the sense of cleanliness. That's because teeth are coated with a pellicle membrane, made of mucus. Roll your tongue over your teeth and you can feel it. Now claim that this film is foul—remember, this is the early 1920s when the germ theory of disease is just taking hold—and you capture the prevention market.

Here is Hopkins, now writing in his Heisenberg scientific mode, telling how he came across the pellicle membrane.

> To advertise a tooth paste this writer has also read many volumes of scientific matter dry as dust. But in the middle of one volume he found the idea which has helped make millions for that tooth paste maker. And has made this campaign one of the sensations of advertising [Hopkins 1991, 272].

There it was, hidden in full view, what he was to call the "cloudy film," the "dingy film" that hides your inner radiance.

After a series of ads in which he focused on how millions of germs are breeding right now in that film, he adds the turbo charger. Brush your teeth with Pepsodent, remove that "viscous coating," and you will make yourself attractive—that is, improve your sex life.

Of course, he doesn't say exactly that. In fact, he may not even be aware that that is what he is doing. Remember, this is just before the days of headlines like "For skin you love to touch" from Woodbury Soap, or "Blow some my way" from Chesterfield cigarettes. But if you look at this ad, the one that pulled more coupons than any of his others, you can see the invocation of romance happening right before your eyes. The sex appeal is all tied up in the illustration and the seemingly bizarre headline, "*Magic* lies in pretty teeth."

Should you doubt, simply check the visual mnemonic, the picture of the young elegants out for the evening. Her cocked head, her laced fingertips, her sparkling smile (to say nothing of her decolleté) is bringing that dashing man of power (who looks a bit like the Arrow collar man) under her influence. Hopkins took great care with illustrations. She is flashing what will become known as "the Pepsodent smile." Still today you can hear the description applied to the likes of Doris Day or Tom Cruise. This smile is doing its job. The young flapper has her man where she wants him, and it is indeed like magic.

Never underestimate the power of magic. It lies at the heart of all advertising. In addressing his colleagues at a convention of advertising agencies many years after this ad, another great advertising genius, Leo Burnett, said it this way:

> After all the meetings are over, the phones have stopped ringing
> and the vocalizing has died down, somebody finally has to get
> out an ad, often after hours. Somebody has to stare at a blank

piece of paper. This is probably the very height of lonesomeness. Out of the recesses of his mind must come words which interest, words which persuade, words which inspire, words which sell. Magic words. I regard him as the man of the hour in our business today [in Simpson 1964, 83].

Hopkins knew that the scientific principle of not just advertising but also of all life was magic. He knew that advertising shared deep and profound similarities with another magical system, religion. Hopkins entered advertising after suffering a profound teenage disillusion with preaching. He had come from a long line of impoverished Scottish Presbyterian and hardshell Baptist preachers. His father had been a Baptist minister, and his mother had encouraged her son to follow him. But when he did preach, he was compelled to tell the truth. Naturally, his preaching days were numbered and his career as a clergyman was short-lived.

The hoary comparison of advertising with religion is as felicitous as it may be trite. Hopkins was one of the first to recognize that advertising was becoming the gospel of redemption in the fallen world of capitalism, that advertising was becoming the vulgate of the secular belief in the redemption of commerce. But how is this order and salvation effected? By magical thinking, pure and simple.

The most magical power of magic is that it is so resolutely denied as the major organizer of meaning. It is so unscientific! We may acknowledge all manner of nefarious magic and have special names for it: black magic, sorcery, voodoo, witchcraft, and necromancy. But what we overlook is theurgy, or white magic. When the harried housewife in the modern ad for Palmolive tells Madge the manicurist that soaking her hands in dish soap has made them feel so great that "it's black magic," Madge corrects her. Madge says, "It's *real* magic." And she is right.

At about the same time Hopkins was experimenting with the pulling power of various headlines, Sir James Frazer had just finished publishing his magisterial *The Golden Bough: A Study in Magic and Religion*. One of the best books ever on advertising, *The Golden Bough* is a rich compendium of the theoretical and practical magic that makes up our reality. Theoretical magic has to do with how we understand the heavens, weather, tides, and cycles of planets. It is the province of religion. It governs our far-off concerns such as what we see when we look up, or how we feel when we think about death.

The practical kind of magic, however, occurs when we cast our eyes downward and contemplate ourselves and the objects around us. Frazer divides the practical, or nearby, magic into the *contagious* and the *imitative*. The contagious is the basis of all testimonial advertising—the explanation of the importance of celebrity endorsement—and has its religious counterparts in such matters as the relics of Christ. If you use this product, if you touch this stone, if you go to this holy place, if you repeat this word, you will be empowered because the product, stone, place, or word has been used by one more powerful than you. Imitative magic, on the other hand, is a variation of *post hoc, ergo propter hoc* thinking. Because the product is made of something, you will be like that thing if you consume it. So Asians use the powder of rhino horns, the Japanese crave certain mollusks, and we deodorize our bodies and then apply musk (from the Sanskrit for testicle) perfume.

This, then, is the magic Hopkins promises for the users of Pepsodent. What is so revolutionary about the headline is not just that Hopkins, who always claimed that truth must be at the heart of successful selling, so baldly used an empty promise of magical results, but also that this promise "pulled" more responses than his other, more rational headlines. The scientific discovery of the profoundly unscientific nature of human desire!

The powerful allure of religion and advertising is the same: magical thinking. Life will make meaning. We will be rescued. This act of rescue, be it effected by the Man from Glad or the Man from Galilee, transports us to the Promised Land of resolution. We will find the peace that passeth understanding, or at least have a sex life. What Pepsodent will rescue us from is not the fiery devil, but the "dingy film" that ruins a young person's life. Use Pepsodent and you will enter what Hopkins calls "a new dental era."

So what happened to Pepsodent and the "new dental era"? It got elbowed aside by a more powerful claim. Remember the little Norman Rockwell shaver coming home from the dentist with his report card? "Look, Ma, no cavities," he says, and in so doing undid all the magic Hopkins had created. The science of medicine trumps the science of magic.

In the 1950s, toothpastes gained a new claim, the so-called secret ingredient. Gleem had GL-70, Ipana had WD-9, and Colgate had Gardol (which placed an "invisible shield" around your teeth that was just like new-age plastics). Crest went them one better. Crest had stannous fluoride, which they called Fluoristan. Better yet, it had the American Dental Association's seal of approval and hence could say, as it did on more than a few occasions, that Crest is an "effective decay-preventive dentifrice when used in a conscientiously applied program of oral hygiene and regular professional care." What could be more scientific than that?

Good-bye, Pepsodent. Although Hopkins's legacy of the dingy film continued in the jingle "You'll wonder where the yellow went / When you brush your teeth with Pepsodent," the modern coupon, the universal product code (the bar-code symbol on packaging that is scanned at the checkout counter), also spelled doom. This product doesn't move off the shelf. Lever Brothers, which now owns the paste, has allowed it to enter the dim half-world of "ghost brands." Pepsodent now sits in benign neglect along with such once-well-advertised venerables as Prell, Ajax, Vitalis, Post Toasties, Viceroy, Carling Black Label, and Yuban.... In the trade they are often called Elvis brands; you think they are dead, but they keep coming back. Perhaps Pepsodent is still hanging on because there are a few people around who can remember when it used to have ... the Magic.

LISTERINE

Gerard Lambert and Selling the Need

HAS THERE EVER BEEN an ad so deliriously nasty as this? Like a baby robin, the youngster looks up to her caregiver for tenderness and gets a whiff of foul breath instead. The body copy makes clear that here is yet another case of "a young woman, who in spite of her personal charm and beauty, never seemed to hold men friends." The quizzical child, however, appears determined to confront what her spinster aunt is ashamed of: Auntie is "broadcasting bad breath." No wonder the men stay away. Dreaded halitosis has gotten in the way of love.

How could this have happened? The tale of Listerine is unique in advertising history not because it was so different, but because it has been so successful for so long. Here is one of the first times that advertising really did create a "cure." But, of course, to make the cure, they first had to create the disease. Listerine did not make mouthwash as much as it made halitosis. Or, in advertising terms, you don't sell the product, you sell the need.

Wisk's "ring around the collar" and Cascade's "water spots" are what motivational psychologists call *constructive discontents*. We are persuaded not so much to buy a product as to remove some dissonance and reestablish a perceived equilibrium. It just so happens that the product stands foursquare in the path of recovery from the contrived affliction. To be sure, this is nothing but a protection racket, as the company selling you the relief is also the one creating the deficiency. But advertising did not invent this kind of persuasion. Religions have been doing it for generations. Modern advertising just perfected it.

If You Want the Truth—Go to a Child: **Copy by Milton Feasley, campaign by Gerard Lambert, halitosis by Listerine, 1924.**

"If you want the truth—

—go to a child." And the old saying is certainly true, isn't it?

Here was the case of a young woman who, in spite of her personal charm and beauty, never seemed to hold men friends.

For a long, long time she searched her mind for the reason. It was a tragic puzzle in her life.

Then one day her little niece told her.

* * *

You, yourself, rarely know when you have halitosis (unpleasant breath). That's the insidious thing about it. And even your closest friends won't tell you.

Sometimes, of course, halitosis comes from some deep-seated organic disorder that requires professional advice. But usually—and fortunately—halitosis is only a local condition that yields to the regular use of Listerine as a mouth wash and gargle. It is an interesting thing that this well-known antiseptic that has been in use for years for surgical dressings, possesses these unusual properties as a breath deodorant. It puts you on the safe and polite side.

Listerine halts food fermentation in the mouth and leaves the breath sweet, fresh and clean. The entire mouth feels invigorated.

Get in the habit of using Listerine every morning and night. And between times before social and business engagements. It's the fastidious thing to do. *Lambert Pharmacal Company, St. Louis, Missouri.*

For HALITOSIS use LISTERINE

If you go into your bathroom, you will see that almost every product there has been introduced into common use by generating constructive discontent. Body odor came from Lifebuoy soap; athlete's foot came from Absorbine Jr.; "five o'clock shadow" from Gillette; tooth film from Pepsodent; and split ends from Alberto VO5. Americans today spend almost $4 billion a year on products whose only purpose is to alter natural body odors, odors unsmelled a generation ago! Teeth, hair, mouth, beard, skin, underarms, you name it, if you can feel anxious about it, it is dealt with in the bathroom. This is the only room in the house that always has a door and almost always has a lock.

The bathroom itself is probably the most revolutionary architectural development in the twentieth century, as much a creation of the need for privacy as for the advertised need to deal with the private self. It is there, behind closed doors, that we go to ritually consume products to cure problems created for the public on the television screen and on the magazine page. While the Victorian parlor (where we used to meet others) has shrunk out of sight, the modern bathroom (where we minister to the ailing self) has grown steadily larger.

The story of how this came to pass starts with Listerine.

At the end of the nineteenth century, Joseph Lister developed a surgical antiseptic. It was quite potent, however, and could only be used with great care lest it damage the surrounding tissue. An American named Jordan Wheat Lambert synthesized a less powerful version and journeyed to England to asked Lister if he could use the already famous name for the product. Lister was flattered and said yes. Lambert added the "ine" suffix which liquefied the product while also making it sound scientific.

Lambert's Listerine was used not just for such minor surgical procedures as sterilizing gauze bandages, but also for any kind of cleaning operation. So it soon became a floor cleaner, an after-shave, a nasal douche, a cure for gonorrhea, even a scalp treatment for dandruff and baldness.

Inevitably it was discovered that Listerine was also good at killing oral germs. So in 1895 it was marketed to the dental profession, and in 1914 it became one of the first prescription products to be sold over the counter. (It still carries the American Dental Association's seal of approval.) But no hint of use as a mouth deodorant.

That's because there was no such thing as bad breath. To be sure, people with various diseases, bad teeth, and so on, had unpleasant mouth odor, but it was not considered socially offensive. Recall that until the 1920s, most Americans bathed only once a week (on Saturday night in anticipation of the Sabbath), and that hair was rarely washed. Soap, still made of animal fats, often smelled worse than body odor!

Gerard, one of Jordan Lambert's sons, went about acquiring such a smell preference, not for himself, but for the rest of us.

In the early 1900s Jordan and his wife died, leaving Lambert Pharmacal to their four sons. Gerard proved a young man of mercurial tastes. For instance, after having spent a few days at Yale University, he decided he didn't like the buildings. He transferred to Princeton. There he majored in the good life, gaining a small measure of campus fame by being chauffeured between classes— a trip of a hundred yards. One thing led to another and he was soon married, father of three children, and $700,000 in debt (thanks to an investment in Arkansas real estate near the current Whitewater development).

Time to get a job, and no better place than at the family factory in St. Louis. His relatives were hardly pleased to see the return of the profligate, but they were soon mollified. Gerard proved to be a business genius, the Arkansas deal notwithstanding. He saved millions in taxes by adding the alcohol to Listerine (it was then about 25 percent hooch) at the bonded distillery instead of at the factory. He cut out the middleman for such simple supplies as corks, and he had the perspicacity actually to talk with the people who wrote the product advertising.

In fact, he summoned the two copywriters, Milton Fuessle and Gordon Seagrove, from Chicago to talk about what they were doing—which was not much. Although the mouth was certainly known as a haven for germs, no one had really concentrated on breath as a symptom of disease. As the three men were discussing the possibility of breath as an "advertising hook," Lambert called for the company chemist:

> When he came into our room, I asked him if Listerine was good for bad breath. He excused himself for a moment and came back with a big book of newspaper clippings. He sat in a chair and I stood looking over his shoulder. He thumbed through the immense book.
>
> "Here it is, Gerard. It says in this clipping from the *British Lancet* that in cases of halitosis…" I interrupted, "What is halitosis?" "Oh," he said, "that is the medical term for bad breath."
>
> [The chemist] never knew what had hit him. I bustled the poor old fellow out of the room. "There," I said, "is something to hang our hat on" [Lambert 1956, 97–98].

As it turned out, he hung more than his hat on halitosis. Lambert hung the entire company on it. He poured money into putting halitosis into every American mouth. Lambert made a pledge to increase his advertising each month by the same percentage as the increase of his sales. He claimed he would stop this only when sales leveled off.

For as long as he owned the company, they never did. From 1922 to 1929 earnings rose from $115,000 to more than $8 million. By the time of the stock-market crash, Listerine was one of the largest buyers of magazine and newspaper space, spending more than $5 million—almost the exact amount of yearly profits. In all that time the product's price, package, and formula had not changed a whit.

Once he found out that the halitosis claim was four times as effective as all others, Lambert focused with pit-bull persistence. All other claims were relinquished. The germ-free mouth belonged to Listerine just as the deodorized underarm belonged to Odorono, the perfumed skin to Palmolive (made from vegetable oils, not animal fats), the shaved face to Gillette, and the "fresh and clean" foot to Mennen talcum powder.

It was no simple process to "own" the mouth. In fact, Lambert left St. Louis for New York and set up shop with Milton Fuessle. The agency was called Lambert & Feasley. Gerard made his colleague change his name (thinking Feasley sounded better than Fuessle), and after Fuessle died, he brought Gordon Seagrove from Chicago to finish the job. For six years he never changed the campaign, only the renditions.

Lambert made it a point never even to retouch any of the photographic images that made up the halitosis campaign. Although he would do minor experiments, as with "If you want the truth—go to a child," his usual targets were young adults in the preparenting stages of life. Who can forget Edna, "whose case was really a pathetic one. Like every woman, her primary ambition was to marry." We see her kneeling before her bureau, clutching the wedding garments that would never be worn. The headline announces the price of halitosis: "Often a Bridesmaid but Never a Bride."

The setting of the standard Listerine ad is just at the age of matrimony. One or the other young eligible is having to deal with the problem that "even your best friend won't tell you" about: "Could I be happy with him in spite of *that?*", "Don't fool yourself, it [halitosis] ruins romance," or the simple "Halitosis

ABOVE: *Often a Bridesmaid but Never a Bride* OPPOSITE: *Halitosis Makes You Unpopular* and *Could I Be Happy With Him in Spite of That?*: The hard sell and halitosis find a home in the 1920s.

makes you unpopular." The copy style—called "whisper copy" in the 1930s—is always the same, a mimic of *True Story* advice to the lovelorn.

Lambert knew his niche because he was a stickler for testing. All his advertising was carefully screened using coupons or store receipts. He would send boxcar loads of Listerine off to some town in midstate Iowa and upstate Maine, run a saturation series of test ads, carefully correlate the results, and then launch nationwide. He would try anything. During the Depression he suggested that halitosis was a reason for firing workers. During Prohibition he thought that alcohol content should be stressed. The company developed what he called "saw-toothed" campaigns in which they would drench, and then quickly remove, advertising until Lambert determined how long short-term memory would last, and which pitches would work best.

Halitosis makes *you unpopular*

"Could I be happy with him in spite of *that?*"

Lambert hated salesmen; they just got in the way of advertising. He never employed more than six, and was fond of saying that the only man he had ever fired was a sales manager. Worse still, salespeople were always tinkering with the retailer's price and display of product. Gerard's aim was to get the end-user into the pharmacy, demand the brand name, and then stomp out if not satisfied.

It is hard to assess Gerard Lambert's genius fairly. It looks so easy, but it was a combination of staking a claim on a body part, of knowing how to use constructive discontent (shame) as a selling tool, of realizing the power of research, and then of hammering it home. Although Lambert is almost always disparaged as "the man who made millions from halitosis," his later life shows it was not luck alone.

Lambert's real contribution may someday be acknowledged. Although he did a stint as CEO of Gillette (while waiting for his divorce to go through), where he introduced the famous Blue Blades, wrote some middling murder mysteries, and innovated with tax-free funding for low-cost public housing, his real talent was in realizing the power of opinion surveys. During World War II he developed techniques to help understand the psychological resistance to various military campaigns. After the war he offered his expertise (usually neglected) to help Tom Dewey, Wendell Willkie, and later Dwight David Eisenhower.

From his home base in Princeton, he befriended George Gallup, funded polling experiments through numerous academic and governmental agencies, and provided seed money for the Institute for International Social Research. A man well ahead of his time, Gerard understood the power of consumer-based positioning. In the stock market he never fought the tape, in marketing he never fought the consumer, and in polling he never second-guessed opinions.

When you look back on Gerard's Listerine advertising, you see that he succeeded almost too well. In retrospect, perhaps Listerine was too well positioned. By creating the mouth as a cauldron of antisocial germs that could be tamed only by strong medicine, Lambert left open the possibility that competing claims could be staked out. In the 1960s, Procter & Gamble's Scope did just that. Scope positioned itself as the feels-good, tastes-great, smells-terrific mouthwash that—in the spirit of the times—"had it all."

Meanwhile Warner-Lambert was left with Lambert's legacy of "medicine breath." Although they have tried to battle back with a new generation of Cool Mint Listerine (blue) and Freshburst Listerine (green), the tough-guy claims of the amber-bottle parent remain. The heritage of "tastes bad, but it's good for you," "kills germs that cause bad breath," and "the taste people hate twice a day" is as deep as anything in American culture. Amazingly, an unprecedented 99 percent of all mouthwash users have tried Original Listerine. That's now the problem: If Listerine excelled by convincing consumers that mouthwash must taste bad to work good, what can a good-tasting Listerine do?

Gerard ran into the same conundrum in the 1930s. He tried to introduce Listerine toothpaste—a sensible enough flanker brand that Warner-Lambert has still not been able to give up. But, alas, his customers could not accept bad taste as a prerequisite for clean teeth. So far no one has figured out a way to position the customer on the horns of this dilemma. But as for bad breath, at least for a while, Gerard Lambert was able to manufacture the horns of a dilemma and then sell the horn-removal equipment.

THE QUEENSBORO CORPORATION

Advertising on the First Electronic Medium

ON MONDAY, August 18, 1922, M. H. Blackwell stood before a microphone at WEAF in New York City. It was 5:15 in the afternoon. He would speak for fifteen minutes and it would cost him fifty dollars. What he said was to be the "mayday" distress call of high culture.

Here is how he was introduced:

> This afternoon the radio audience is to be addressed by Mr. Blackwell of the Queensboro Corporation who will say a few words concerning Nathaniel Hawthorne and the desirability of fostering the helpful community spirit and the healthful, unconfined home life that were Hawthorne's ideals. Ladies and gentlemen: Mr. Blackwell.

After reminding the audience that it was just fifty-eight years since Nathaniel Hawthorne had died, Mr. Blackwell noted that the Queensboro Corporation had named its most recent development "Hawthorne Court" in the writer's honor. Then came the slow-moving pitch:

> I wish to thank those within sound of my voice for the broadcasting opportunity afforded me to urge this vast radio audience to seek the recreation and the daily comfort of the home removed from the congested part of the city, right at the boundaries of God's great outdoors, and within a few miles by subway from the business section of Manhattan. This sort of residential environ-

ment strongly influenced Hawthorne, America's greatest writer of fiction. He analyzed with charming keenness the social spirit of those who had thus happily selected their homes, and he painted the people inhabiting those homes with good-natured relish.

One cannot help but notice that Mr. Blackwell, who may have had a perceptive sense of urban angst, had little sense of Nathaniel Hawthorne. I daresay he'd never read a word of "America's *greatest* writer of fiction" (what of Twain, James, Poe, Melville?). And how one could read *The Scarlet Letter*, *The House of Seven Gables*, or any of the short stories and think that Hawthorne had anything but a high level of nervous anxiety about the happy home life of American suburbanites? The only happy people in Hawthorne's miasmic world are loonies and crackpots.

But, no matter, Blackwell had made the romantic connection between the good life and the natural life, and he had "laid the pipe" between suburban space and family happiness. Now he upped the ante:

> Let me enjoin upon you as you value your health and your hopes and your home happiness, get away from the solid masses of brick, where the meager opening admitting a slant of sunlight is mockingly called a light shaft, and where children grow up starved for a run over a patch of grass and the sight of a tree.
>
> Apartments in congested parts of the city have proved failures. The word "neighbor" is an expression of peculiar irony—a daily joke.
>
> Thousands of dwellers in the congested district apartments want to remove to healthier and happier sections but they don't know and they can't seem to get into the belief that their living situation and home environment can be improved. Many of them balk at buying a house in the country or the suburbs and becoming a commuter. They have visions of toiling down in a cellar

with a sullen furnace, or shoveling snow, or of blistering palms pushing a clanking lawn mower. They can't seem to overcome the pessimistic inertia that keeps pounding into their brains that their crowded, unhealthy, unhappy living conditions cannot be improved....

Those who balk at building a house or buying one already built need not remain deprived of the blessings of the home within the ideal residential environment, or the home surrounded by social advantages and the community benefits where neighbor means more than a word of eight letters....

Let me close by urging that you hurry to the apartment home near the green fields and the neighborly atmosphere right on the subway without the expense and trouble of a commuter, where health and community happiness beckon—the community life and the friendly environment that Hawthorne advocated [in Archer 1928, 397–98].

Three weeks later the Queensboro Corporation had sold all its property in Hawthorne Court in Jackson Heights in present-day Queens.

No one had predicted this. In fact, the one thing that had been predicted about radio was that it would *not* become an advertising medium. It was going to be an educational medium—the university of the air. Secretary of Commerce Herbert Hoover had assured all that it was "inconceivable that we should allow so great a possibility for service ... to be drowned in advertising chatter" and that if important messages ever "became the meat in a sandwich of two patent medicine advertisements, it would destroy broadcasting."

Besides, at the same time Mr. Blackwell was speaking, Cyrus Curtis was selling 2 million weekly copies of his *Saturday Evening Post* and pocketing some $28 million in advertising revenues—astounding figures for those times. Curtis had claimed that once he got a circulation of 400,000, he could afford to give the magazine away to anyone who would pay postage. He was right. The magazine grew so plump on advertising that it was bought, newly published but undistributed, as scrap paper. By December 7, 1929, the *Post* weighed in at two pounds. Its 272 pages contained twenty-one hours of reading matter, showcased 214 national advertisers, and took in ad revenue of $1,512,000.

Nothing would rival such magazines, with their glossy pictures, as an advertising medium, certainly not a medium made up only of sound. So it would be up to radio to transmit the best that had been thought and said. Radio would be verbal, intellectual, rational, even ponderous. It would open the floodgates between the government and its people, between the universities and their students. In fact, almost half of the first licenses for early radio stations were granted to universities, whether they wanted them or not.

Sound familiar? Just a few years ago the Internet was going to be a conduit carrying a never-ending supply of knowledge from the centers of power and learning out to the most distant monitor. The World Wide Web was most definitely *not* going to be filled with blinking banners and "click on me! click on me!" icons. This new medium was going to improve, to lift, to make better, to civilize. There is no need for me to recite the most popular Web sites and who sponsors them.

Mr. Blackwell's fifteen minutes of no fame generated $27,000 in sales for the Queensboro Corporation, and in so doing pretty well sealed the fate of radio, television, and now the World Wide Web. While it took about twenty years for radio to become colonized by commercial interests, television never had a chance. The Web went in months.

Radio was the first electronic medium. No one knew what to do with it. Just as today our kids spend countless hours "surfing the Web," and just as those of us over fifty years old concentrated on the unblinking Indian in the center of the video test pattern, our grandparents dedicated their quality time to turning the dial trying to hear something—anything!—of even minimal interest. What they heard before Mr. Blackwell was a mishmash of religious, educational, sports, and government programming, all jumbled up on the same frequencies.

What they heard in the decades after Mr. Blackwell was a highly organized broadcast day supported by commercial interests, each trying to reach the widest possible audience.

The history of radio is instructive. Radio started because, at the outbreak of World War I, the navy needed to communicate with ships at sea (the *Titanic* tragedy in 1912 might have been avoided had wireless operators been on duty), and the army needed a way to direct troops in the trenches (using barbed wire as antennae). The problem was that too many separate patents were in too many corporate hands. Rather than nickel-and-dime the patents loose, the Justice Department essentially stripped them from private industry and repackaged them inside a consortium called the "Radio Group"—later the Radio Corporation of America.

The war over, national interest no longer a concern, RCA went on its merry way. Patent holders realized there was more money to be made by staying together than in breaking apart. Nobody asked for patents back. However, Westinghouse, one of the dispossessed patent holders, had made a pile of radio stuff—tubes, amplifiers, transmitters, crystal receivers, and the like—that it needed to unload. So in November 1920, Westinghouse started KDKA in Pittsburgh on the *Field of Dreams* principle—"Build it and they will come." It worked. Once transmitters were built, the surplus receiving apparatus could be unloaded.

You could even make a radio receiver at home. All you needed was a spool of wire, a crystal, an aerial, and earphones—all produced by Westinghouse. Patience and a cylindrical oatmeal box were supplied by the hobbyist. By July 1922, four hundred "volunteer" stations had sprung up.

People didn't seem to care what was on, as long as they were receiving *something*. When stereophonic sound was introduced in the 1950s, the most popular records were not of music, but of the ordinary sounds of locomotives and cars passing from speaker to speaker. People on the East Coast used to marvel at television pictures of waves breaking in California, just as monks undoubtedly stood in awe in front of the first printed letters. Bleary-eyed Junior, now glued to the computer screen, is only the most recent evolutionary development of ancient awe made electronic.

The problem with radio was that everyone was broadcasting on the same wavelength. When transmitters were placed too close together, the signals became mixed and garbled. By 1927 there were so many broadcasters that they petitioned Congress to help them sort out the airwaves. By 1934 Congress updated the law by passing a full-fledged Communications Act, which established the Federal Communications Commission.

Ever eager to help out, AT&T suggested a solution. Their New York subsidiary already had a hub station, WEAF (for Wind, Earth, Air, Fire) in Manhattan, and they would link stations together using their already-in-place phone lines. Soon everyone would hear clearly. They envisioned tying some thirty-eight stations together in a system they called "toll broadcasting." The word "toll" was the tip-off. Someone was going to have to pay. The phone company suggested that time could be sold to private interests and they called this subsidy "ether advertising."

Broadcasters had tried all kinds of innovative things, even broadcasting live from a football stadium and a dance floor, to gather an audience, so "ether advertising" didn't seem so revolutionary. Why not let companies buy time to talk about their products, especially if such talk was done in good taste? It wasn't really advertising: no mention of where the products were, no samples offered, no store locations, no comparisons, no price information, and never, ever, during the "family hour" (from 7:00 to 11:00 P.M.)—just a few words about what it is that you offer. In return, listeners got clear sound "free."

Ma Bell knew she had something attractive. But she just couldn't get the mice to come out for the cheese. Ad agencies wouldn't bite. Why should they pay the toll? The monies from "ether advertising" were all going to the long-lines division of the phone company. So AT&T did the only sensible thing. The company offered the same 15-percent commission that the agencies got for buying print space just for sending business their way. The agencies got the money (soon called a rebate) even if they didn't prepare a word of copy! Not to put too fine a point on it, AT&T essentially bribed the agencies. They even provided the announcer for free.

Whereas Westinghouse thought that you used broadcasting to sell radio sets, AT&T knew that the big money was to be made in delivering listeners to advertisers. Agencies soon fell in line. William Rankin, an adman, bought one hundred minutes of time to discuss Mineralava moisturizing soap, just to see if radio was for real. The product flew off the shelves. Consumers bought the soap simply because they had heard about it on the radio. No one today knows why the phrase "As Seen on TV" is a motivation to purchase, but here is where the phenomenon starts. Somehow we make the connection between a product being advertised and a product being worthy as one and the same. Soon Rankin enlisted his other clients, like Goodrich and Gillette, to have a go at *broad-casting* their message. Others followed.

The most pressing problem for advertisers was to find out what listeners wanted to hear. The Universities of the Air were under-enrolled, to say the least. By the late 1920s, agencies had found out what gathered an audience. The public wanted music, all right, but not classical music. They wanted to hear a new kind of music you could dance to, swing and sway to. This popular music, which centered around well-known "hits," elbowed aside classical music, which was too long and undanceable. The audience for "long-hair" music just sat there. But the audience for popular music wanted to be active. Not only was this short-hair music exciting to the young (who were starting to be the prime consumers), but advertisers could attach their clients' names to the players—something you couldn't do with the New York Symphony and the Metropolitan Opera.

So there was the Goodrich Silvertown Orchestra, the Cliquot Club Eskimos, the Gold Dust Twins, the Ipana Troubadours, the A&P Gypsies, and the Kodak Chorus. Alas, this "gratitude factor" or "indirect selling" didn't do more than put your name "out there." It didn't *sell* your product. What it was really selling was popular music.

And popular music was creating an uproar. Rather like smut on the Internet today, boogie tunes were clearly not what was expected of this medium. So what about those universities? Weren't they supposed to make sure the airwaves would be full of "the best that had been thought and said"? Weren't they supposed to keep the greedy fingers of advertisers out of the pie and these carnal sounds off the airwaves?

While there were more than ninety educational stations (out of a total 732) in 1927, by the mid-1930s there were only a handful. What happened? The university stations had sold their licenses to a new breed of executives who saw that the big money in radio would come from advertisers. These executives, like William Paley, the urbane impresario of CBS, had been merging individual stations into networks—called "nets" or, better yet, "webs"—emanating from Manhattan. ABC, NBC, and CBS were the results of this consolidation.

In one of the few attempts to recapture cultural control from commercial exploitation, the National Educational Association in the early 1930s lobbied Senators Robert Wagner of New York and Henry Hatfield of West Virginia to reshuffle the stations and restore a quarter of them to university hands. These stations would forever be advertising-free, making "sweetness and light" available to all. The lobbying power of the NEA met the clout of Madison Avenue, and it was no contest. The Wagner-Hatfield bill died aborning, defeated by an almost two-to-one margin.

One of the reasons the bill foundered so quickly was the emergence of a new cultural phenomenon, the country-wide hit show. Never before had an entertainment been developed that an entire nation—by 1937 more than three-quarters of American homes had at least one radio—could experience at the same time. *Amos 'n' Andy* at NBC had shown what a hit show could do. AT&T noted that phone calls dropped 50 percent during the broadcast, and water departments found that pressure decreased just after the show.

But these were not the important registers of concern. Hits could make millions of dollars in advertising revenue. In fact, Pepsodent, the sole sponsor of *Amos 'n' Andy*, saw its fortunes soar with the show's popularity. Although not yet called a "blockbuster" (that would come with the high-explosive bombs of World War II), the effect of a hit was already acknowledged as concussive. Nothing would stand in its way.

What the hit show really blew up was the myth of the "public" airwaves. Section 304 of the Communications Act makes no mention of public or government ownership. Only regulatory power is sited with the government, not ownership. "Public airwaves" is a catchy phrase, all right, but it's a myth. The airwaves were going to be regulated by the feds, but they were going to be ruled by the highest bidder, and the highest bidder was going to be related to Mr. Blackwell.

So, in a generation, radio became like newspapers and magazines, a medium supported by advertising. In fact, unlike print, radio was soon totally supported by commercial interests.

It's "free" all right, if you don't value your time and attention. When television appeared in the late 1940s, all that was added was moving pictures. The Internet and Web TV increased speed and greater audience control. But Mr. Blackwell is still there, behind the winking pixels, picking up the tab and banking on renting your attention for just another "word from our sponsor."

THE KID IN UPPER 4

The Birth of Advocacy Advertising

MOST OF THE TIME, advertising does just what it claims to do. It draws attention (*ad-vert*: to turn toward) to a product. But sometimes advertising tries to draw your attention *away* from the product.

Advertising starts in earnest in the nineteenth century as producers start to pile up large surpluses that they cannot profitably sell. Like the sorcerer's apprentice, machines don't know when enough is enough, so advertising becomes the sorcerer's agent trying to distribute the mess the apprentice has produced. "Here, look at this one-of-a-kind product," the adman says, trying to hide the fact that thousands of these things are pouring out of the factory.

Innovations in advertising usually happen when surpluses are most out of control. Salesmen always make the most interesting deals when beads of flop sweat start to appear. New media are colonized, new selling techniques are tried out, and creativity—whatever that may be—becomes not just prized but a necessity.

So the first question in advertising history is, When do the most unruly surpluses occur? The answer is simple: After war. From the Civil War on, the first rule of victory is that the winner is the side that can produce the most war material. To the victor go the spoils. The problem is that often the spoils are now pretty worthless. Ironically, the winner is stuck holding the bag of machine-made blankets, boots, ball bearings, bazookas.... A call is soon made to the men on Madison Avenue.

The most creative times in advertising culture were just after the Civil War in the North with the rise of magazine culture, and

The Kid in Upper 4 by Nelson Metcalf Jr.: "Exvertisement" for the New Haven Railroad, 1942.

THE KID IN UPPER 4

It is 3:42 a.m. on a troop train.

Men wrapped in blankets are breathing heavily.

Two in every lower berth. One in every upper.

This is no ordinary trip. It may be their last in the U.S.A. till the end of the war. Tomorrow they will be on the high seas.

One is wide awake . . . listening . . . staring into the blackness.

It is the kid in Upper 4.

☆   ☆   ☆

Tonight, he knows, he is leaving behind a lot of little things—and big ones.

The taste of hamburgers and pop . . . the feel of driving a roadster over a six-lane highway . . . a dog named Shucks, or Spot, or Barnacle Bill.

The pretty girl who writes so often . . . that gray-haired man, so proud and awkward at the station . . . the mother who knit the socks he'll wear soon.

Tonight he's thinking them over.

There's a lump in his throat. And maybe —a tear fills his eye. *It doesn't matter, Kid. Nobody will see . . . it's too dark.*

☆   ☆   ☆

A couple of thousand miles away, where he's going, they don't know him very well.

But people all over the world are waiting, praying for him to come.

And he will come, this kid in Upper 4.

With new hope, peace and freedom for a tired, bleeding world.

☆   ☆   ☆

Next time you are on the train, remember the kid in Upper 4.

If you have to stand enroute—it is so he may have a seat.

If there is no berth for you—it is so that he may sleep.

If you have to wait for a seat in the diner —it is so he . . . and thousands like him . . . may have a meal they won't forget in the days to come.

For to treat him as our most honored guest is the least we can do to pay a mighty debt of gratitude.

THE NEW HAVEN R.R.

★ SERVING THE GREAT INDUSTRIAL STATES OF MASSACHUSETTS, RHODE ISLAND AND CONNECTICUT then immediately after both the World Wars with the explosion of first radio, then television.

Conversely, the most boring times in advertising are *usually* times of dearth. No surplus equals no reward for creative advertising. When the war machine is draining production from the civilian sector, advertising agents start reminiscing about the good old days and creating ads like "There's a Ford in Your Future."

Advertisers get anxious during two events: economic depressions and wartime. In economic hard times the first business expense to get cut is advertising—ironic, because you'd think that businesses would increase advertising, if advertising really worked as advertised. And during wartime, governments begin to question the function of advertising for frivolous items and wonder about its deductibility as a necessary expense.

As the war in Europe raged, President Truman mentioned the unmentionable: advertising costs should be deleted as a deductible business expense, or at least reduced, because there was no need to advertise. No surplus equals no need to advertise. Mention to an adman what would happen if tax laws treated advertising as extraneous, and you will see pure panic. Same for businessmen. Given a choice between paying taxes and using those monies to buy advertising, albeit worthless advertising, most executives would choose the latter. At least such advertising can make the company feel good about itself.

As a consequence, the agencies offered to turn their attention to the war effort if Truman would turn his elsewhere. The War Advertising Council encouraged the purchasing of war bonds, the donating of blood, the thrill of enlistment, and, most interesting in terms of how they would later behave, the encouragement of women to enter the workforce. All *pro bono,* as the modern reincarnation of the War Council, the Ad Council, likes to say, almost truthfully.

At the same time, to protect their billings, the agencies encouraged their clients, plump with cash that they did not want

taxed as "excess profits," to continue to buy media space and fill it
at least with high-minded, altruistic advertising. Needless to say,
the agencies still collected their 15 percent for this contribution.

Most of the war advertising did not go into print, since paper
was a crucial war material. Most of it went into radio. GM supported the NBC Orchestra, U.S. Rubber backed broadcasts of the
New York Philharmonic, and Allis-Chalmers underwrote the
Boston Symphony. Therefore the war advertising we see in print is
advertising on its best behavior, treading lightly. It had to accomplish two goals: protect the products of the company and support
the war effort.

That implicit contradiction of being naughty/being nice is what
makes this ad for the New Haven Railroad so interesting. The ad
is not *selling* anything. Just the opposite. It is drawing attention
away from the client's lousy product. And in so doing it opened
the door for a whole new genre of advertising, advocacy advertising, placed by companies that have misbehaved ... or worse.

I call them "exvertisements" because they try to get you to
take your eye off the ball. The industry calls them "issue advertising," which does give them a nice tone. Look over here, says the
big chemical company, see how this poor family is cooking with
napalm. The cigarette companies truck the Bill of Rights around
the country as if they own the First Amendment; beer brewers
righteously suggest knowing "when to say when" while the rest of
the time they are telling you that this is "the beer to have when
you are having more than one"; liquor companies advocate equivalent taxation for hard liquor, beer, and wine. The list goes on.

The Ad Council, a confederation of agencies, has even institu-
tionalized the genre, producing such memorable campaigns as "A
Mind Is a Terrible Thing to Waste," "This Is Your Brain on Drugs,"
the Crash Dummies, the Weeping [over pollution] Indian, Smokey
the Bear, and Rosie the Riveter. Detractors are fond of pointing
out that the Ad Council has neglected such problems as birth and

gun control, automotive safety, corporate pollution, and nicotine and alcohol addiction, preferring more client-friendly topics.

Most advocacy is bloodless, but this ad for the New Haven Railroad is different. First, of course, is the guileless artwork. One jot more Norman Rockwell and it would go over the edge. Ed Georgi, the famous illustrator, has just the right composition. The two bottom bunkers (appropriately facing away from each other) are clearly in dreamland, while our young cub looks heavenward, free of all shadows, *yet the light is behind him*. I think this anomaly is a key to unlocking the power of the text.

The text was originally set horizontally, but Nelson Metcalf Jr., who wrote it, says that when he sent a dummy version to the railroad, the advertising manager said there was "something wrong." Metcalf's boss knew the problem. The copy panel needed to be perpendicular to the boys and hence tilted to the reader. This is no small matter, as the ad is asking us to move aside for these boys, to change our point of view, to make allowances. Right from the get-go, we do.

Before we get to the text, a word about the client's problem. The New Haven Railroad always had lousy service, in part because it had two opposing tasks. As the small print at the bottom says, the railroad served the industrial states of Massachusetts, Rhode Island, and Connecticut, but its chief job was as daily schlepper of commuters into Manhattan. So, of course, it had a bad rep among New Englanders who used it as a shuttle service. Now, with the war on, that service was going from bad to worse.

Metcalf, who was fresh from college, was given the assignment: Quiet the complaining suits. Damp down the whining about not getting a seat in the dining car. Make the waiting passengers more patient, make the outraged less eager to berate management. Write an exvertisement.

His small Colton agency in Boston had tried stressing "Right of Way for Fighting Might," in which they argued that expediting freight trumped shunting passengers. They tried "Thunder Along the Line," in which they switched the argument to foreground the long hours and hard work of railroad men. But nothing worked.

Metcalf was undeterred. He vowed he would write an ad that "would make *everybody* who read it *feel ashamed* to complain about train service" (Metcalf 1991, 24; emphasis in original).

The minute you read the text you see why. Here we have the invocation of shame, that most painful of social controls, directed toward whoever had the temerity even to think nasty thoughts, let alone say something, about the crappy service.

Under mawkish sentimentality is pure advertising genius. Note how the slightly patronizing word "kid" in the headline immediately becomes a "man" in the first stanza. (Forgive the poetic jargon on my part, but this ad is really written in blank verse.) Then notice how he is made mythic a few lines later with "*It* is the kid in Upper 4." Then the invocation of the catalog, something as ancient as the Homeric epic. Here's what our Ulysses is leaving behind: hamburgers, hot rod, soda pop, Fido, girlfriend, dad, mom, in ascending order of magnitude.

By the time he reaches "mom," the lump reaches his throat. Metcalf says that the agency secretary put the "lump" in the copy, and it gets to the kid's throat just as it gets to ours.

The bardic voice then quickly finishes off this stanza by letting the kid cry while not losing any dignity. "It doesn't matter, Kid," intrudes the all-knowing narrator. "Nobody will see...." But what is really happening is that we, too, are overpowered with feelings. Synchronicity.

This kid, our kid, my kid, is leaving us. We are saying good-bye to him, in a sense our only begotten son, so that others who have prayed for his arrival may be saved.

You may begin to see what is going on here. This kid is cast as the redeemer, for he, and he alone, is going to bring "new hope, peace, and freedom" to the fallen world, the world tired and bleeding.

Warner Sallman's
Head of Christ.

He will bleed for them, and in so doing he will give them peace. Now you can understand why, although the light is behind his head in the illustration, this lad looks just like the famous version of Christ painted by Warner Sallman. Until the Supreme Court took it down, this image was hung in almost every American school. Sallman's *Head of Christ* was in most every Christian church, in presentation Bibles, on bulletin boards and calendars. Millions of wallet-size reproductions were made for servicemen. Our doughboys carried this image with them and the readers of this ad knew it—although perhaps not consciously.

If there is any doubt what is being invoked, read the last stanza. The text is lifted from countless recitative readings between minister and congregation. Invocation and refrain, exhortation and response. The readers of this ad and the complainers about rail service would have one thing in common: they belonged to a Christian culture that each Sunday practiced a litany that had the same rhythms. Before going to Harvard, Metcalf had prepped at St. Paul's. He knew this stuff by heart.

> If you have to stand enroute—*it is so he may have a seat.*
> If there is no berth for you—*it is so that he may sleep.*

You can hear the ancient echoes of an earlier young man who also suffered that we might be saved. He who is now moving amongst us is more than some kid, he is our "most honored guest," and no gratitude on our part can ever match his sacrifice.

The ad was initially run in November 1942 as a single trial insertion in the *New York Herald Tribune*. Needless to say, it

SUNDAY SCHOOL
INTERMEDIATE TEACHER
JANUARY FEBRUARY MARCH 1947

never stopped running. Elmer Davis, head of the Office of War Information, ordered that it be run in newspapers around the country. Railroad companies and service companies picked it up and sponsored it. The Pennsylvania Railroad asked for permission to make three hundred posters of it for their stations. The text was read on radio stations, pinned to countless bulletin boards, and enclosed in letters. More than eight thousand letters arrived at the New Haven Railroad office.

The "Kid" appeared in *Life, Newsweek, Time,* in an MGM movie short, and as a song. More important for the national interest, however, the ad was used to raise money for the Red Cross, to sell U.S. War Bonds, and by the U.S. Army to build morale among servicemen. After all, this ad made sacrifice into religious ritual.

It also showed advertisers that a good ad can do more than work off surplus; it can tamp down complaints. If only the railroad had run so smoothly.

Head of Christ as popular culture icon in the 1940s.

DE BEERS

A Good Campaign Is Forever

THE PIVOTAL INSIGHT in advertising is "I know that half my advertising dollars are being wasted, I just can't figure out which half." This truism, coined in the late nineteenth century, is attributed to, among others, Lord Leverhume of Lever Brothers and John Wanamaker of the famous Philadelphia department store. It describes the central axiom of sponsored speech: very little of it gets through to the consumer. You still hear the sentiment expressed today, with the percent of waste raised.

This is what makes the N. W. Ayer campaign for De Beers Consolidated Mines Limited so remarkable. For half a century this campaign, selling polished transparent rocks as instruments of romantic love, was probably the least wasteful advertising ever created. Every dollar spent was worth it.

While advertising cannot create demand, it can intercept and reformat desire, and when this happens, watch out! New markets open up overnight. While we usually think of De Beers' dominance as the result of controlling supply, its real achievement has been in manipulating demand. Thanks to Ayer, the South African cartel—which now contributes only 15 percent of supply—has become the most successful monopoly on earth.

Finding rocks is easy. Selling rocks is tough. In the last fifty years two markets have been opened up for stones. You wear them *on* your fingers when you are in love, and you put them *over* the body of a loved one after death. The latter category was mastered by the Rock of Ages Corporation, which captured the monumentality argument and franchised it under the barely disguised

Honeymoon on the Rocky Coast of Maine, painted by Nicolia Cikovsky for De Beers, 1948.

HONEYMOON ON THE ROCKY COAST OF MAINE...
where sea and sun bid welcome. Painted for
the De Beers Collection by Nicolai Cikovsky.

a Diamond is forever

Together, hearts light with love, they've shared their new life's happiness . . .
the church so full of music and of friends, the wedding banquet marked with cake and laughter,
and now, these touched-with-magic days in a world that seems their own.
In the engagement diamond on her finger, a fire is kindled by such joys, to light
their way through future days with hopes and memories. That is why her diamond,
though it need not be costly or of many carats, should be chosen with special
care. Color, cutting and clarity, as well as carat weight, contribute
to its beauty and value. A trusted jeweler is your best adviser.

The price ranges at left were developed for
your guidance through a nationwide independent check among representative jewelers in April, 1949. (Exact weights shown are
infrequent.) Add Federal tax.

De Beers Consolidated Mines, Ltd.

N. W. AYER & SON

aura of religion ("Rock of Ages cleft for me," the Church built on rock, the concept of rock as covenant with God). But at almost the same time that granite memorials were being turned from headstone markers to life testimonials for the common man, diamonds were being positioned as the signifiers of undying love for his life partner.

Was it happenstance that the same war-ravaged generation that responded to these stones was also comforted by the J. Walter Thompson Agency's imaging of Prudential Insurance as the Rock of Gibraltar? In a world perceived as susceptible to monstrosities, there was great comfort in aligning oneself with rocks.

Although the wealthy of both sexes had been accustomed to displaying these colorless crystals, they became an investment commodity in the late nineteenth century. You would buy raw diamonds and put them away for safekeeping. After the Depression, the diamond trade crashed; too many of them came out of safekeeping all at once, and speculators glutted the market. It became clear to the fragmented diamond industry that as long as diamonds were seen as tradable and not as something to buy and hold, the market would always be subject to such wild gyrations.

This is because of a paradox unique to these stones: the very quality that seems to make them so valuable is precisely what must ultimately render them worthless. Not only do they last forever, but diamonds have almost no practical use. All you can do is grind them up and put them on drill bits. Unlike gold or silver, carbon allotropes aren't malleable or electrically conductive; diamonds just sit there and sparkle. If ever the Draconian laws of supply and demand were applied, every diamond dug out of the earth would diminish by so much the value of every still-existing diamond that has preceded it.

All through history, the laws of supply and demand have been held at bay. First they were pushed aside by what were called sumptuary laws. Certain kinds of meats (like the king's deer), beverages (such as exotic teas and coffee), styles of fashionable livery, particular fabrics, rare spices and sweeteners, styles of wigs, places to live, and the like, were simply placed off limits to commoners. Ditto diamonds. These laws against consuming what was called "luxury" used to be administered by the ecclesiastical courts. This was because luxury was defined as living above one's station, a form of insubordination against the concept of "copia"—the idea that God's world is already full and complete.

Though the proffered sins behind such laws were gluttony and greed—luxury objects were by definition *sumptuous*—in truth the prohibitions were social. Sumptuary laws were part of an elaborate symbolic system designed to keep class demarcations in place. We now use excise taxes on cigarettes, expensive automobiles, yachts, liquor, and gasoline, and our purpose is not to separate groups, but to make consuming certain materials a burden.

Diamonds had been such a protected luxury. In fact, until the fifteenth century, only the elites were allowed to display them. Diamonds appeared on royal heads and on top of their scepters as a kind of blinking reminder of who wielded the big stick.

Then, in 1447, Archduke Maximilian of Austria gave a diamond ring to his girlfriend, Mary of Burgundy, placing it on the third finger of her left hand, apparently in honor of the ancient Egyptian belief that the *vena amoris* (vein of love) ran straight from the heart to the tip of that finger. As a distant harbinger of what was to come, the rock was becoming something more than political signage; it was becoming a symbol of amorous intention.

The diamond market was inching away from one maintained by royal and ecclesiastical power to one maintained, as one diamond dealer famously put it, "by the male erection." But the paradox of worthlessness remained: the only value of diamonds is what can be attributed. If diamonds are not a king's best friend, then they have to be made "a girl's best friend."

After World War I, no one was doing the attribution. Diamonds were on their way out. Young swains were promising their undying devotion by giving automobiles, oceanic travel, watches, and fur coats. Other rocks, such as rubies, sapphires, turquoise, opals, topaz, and onyx were more romantic, more colorful, more exotic and erotic than diamonds.

Worse still, vast new fields of diamonds were being discovered in the lands now known as Zaire, Ghana, Namibia, and especially in Botswana. Even bigger fields would be found in the Argyle mines of Australia, bigger ones still in Siberian Russia. Diamonds were anything but rare, and hence lost much of the value they might have had.

Diamond suppliers were facing every producer's worst nightmare: increasing supply, decreasing demand. Three things had to happen: First, and most important, diamonds had to stop being thought of as a commodity. They should be bought, but not sold, like gold or silver, because that would invoke the iron laws of the market. In economic terms, they had to be made unfungible. Second, the diamond had to be tied to some more regular use than sticking in a crown, a scepter, or even in a ring. Diamonds had to be made ritualistic, totemic, metaphoric. They had to be made so meaningful that they could be bought to be given. In other words, the after-market, the secondhand market as it were, had to be destroyed. Buy, buy, buy, but never sell, sell, sell. And, third, to accomplish the first two, the producers had to promise not to deviate from either the controlled supply or the controlled meaning of their product. They had to form a cartel to funnel the rocks down a single channel in only one direction: toward what is known as the buy-hole.

The amazing transformation of diamonds began on September 6, 1938, a full year before the first advertisement appeared, when a partner of a New York bank phoned a vice-president of N. W. Ayer & Son, Inc., to arrange a meeting between the agency and representatives of Ernest Oppenheimer. This first meeting, like all subsequent meetings, had to be carefully arranged. Oppenheimer's firm, De Beers Consolidated Mines, was a cartel, already controlling more than 90 percent of the market. American laws forbid monopolies from having offices on U.S. soil. Hence, almost all future meetings occurred in South Africa or in London, and it was there that budgets were set and campaigns arranged.

N. W. Ayer was the obvious agency to do the job. Not only was it the granddaddy of American agencies, it was also the most "white shoe" of all the major firms. Over the years, Ayer had become staffed by the scions of well-heeled WASPs. The story goes that when paychecks were handed out, they were often dumped into desk drawers and forgotten. These men knew what upper-middle-class women wanted, and it was not more golf clubs.

Better yet, Ayer would keep things quiet, respectful, out of the limelight. In fact, the agency was named N. W. Ayer & Son even though N. W. never participated in the agency. His son, Francis Wayland Ayer, thought the title sounded more established, more genteel.

No doubt about it, the agency was good with difficult products. They had introduced not just the Ford Model T and car travel but also the Ford Tri-Motor plane and air travel; they had sold the National Biscuit Company's products by emphasizing the In-Er-Seal packaging, not the foodstuff; they had launched Camel cigarettes and coined "I'd walk a mile for a Camel"; they positioned coffee as a drink worthy of a "break," and, perhaps most importantly, the agency had created the masterful AT&T campaigns that protected the phone monopoly long after market conditions had warranted new competition.

Ayer would have to be discreet for another reason than the government suspicion of monopolies. Most of these diamonds were coming from South Africa. Everyone knew how Cecil Rhodes had run the Kimberley Mine. It was common knowledge that the "diggers" were treated abominably. You didn't have to be a reader of the *National Geographic* to know how "dry" mining was done, with humans scraping the ground like dogs after bones. And you didn't have to be a reader of *The New York Times* to know how closely this apartheid system was coupled with our own racial past. (Needless to say, Ayer also kept its distance years later when De Beers "lent" our erstwhile enemy, the Soviet Union, more than $1 billion in order to make sure they funneled their diamonds into the cartel's euphemistic Central Selling Organization.)

Before the first ad, Ayer conducted one of the most thorough market studies ever done. Here's what they gleaned from carefully interviewing 2,073 married women, 2,042 married men, 480 college men, and 502 college women. The first postwar generation did not associate diamonds with ritualized engagement to be married, let alone with romantic love. Another problem was that young men were confused about how much to pay, and how big a diamond had to be to satisfy "her concerns." And finally, since no direct sale between De Beers and the end-user could occur (the monopoly problem), the advertising must be done for the entire category, not for the proprietary version.

Category advertising is almost never done. You don't sell biscuits, shoes, cigarettes, automobiles, or computer chips. You sell Ritz, Nike, Marlboro, Chevrolet, or an Intel 586. If everybody's biscuits are in the same barrel, and if they look pretty much the same, it probably doesn't reward you to tell people to buy biscuits. But diamonds are different, thanks to the cartel.

The only sticking point with De Beers was that Ayer insisted that its research showed that men needed to know the exact pricing system before they would bite. You often hear how savvy it was that Harry Winston or Tiffany's would lend their stones to Hollywood stars. Drenching a starlet with brilliant baubles was a way of generating value by association—for both parties. "Diamonds are a girl's best friend," cooed Marilyn Monroe. To the cartel the refrain continues, "Marilyn is diamonds' best friend."

Unfortunately, what the merchants lent with one hand was taken with the other, for while the mechanic's sweetheart may have thought, "I wish I had what Marilyn has," the mechanic thought, "Marilyn is way too expensive for me to afford."

Because men would be doing almost all the buying in America, a practical system had to be concocted that would calm them down and get them safely through the buy-hole. Hence the scientific-sounding voodoo about carat weight, color, cutting, clarity of the stones, *and* prices that invariably appeared in the bottom margin of the early ads. Women looked at the picture and read the body copy of the ad. Men were shown the small print over in the corner of the page.

Prices were only vaguely mentioned. Since De Beers couldn't control what the jeweler charged, they did not want to be confined by advertised prices. Ayer told them not to worry: rigidly control the wholesale prices, remove the after-market, and the small-time, downtown jeweler would fall into line. In fact, Ayer even encouraged local jewelers *not* to advertise because they would only cheapen the process by having competitive sales. Let De Beers advertise for you. In so doing, the cartel essentially sold direct to the consumer.

In a still more clever adaptation, the prices were later removed and stated in terms of wages. "Is two months' salary too much for a diamond engagement ring?" asks one ad. Talk about a rhetorical question!

The next aspect of the Ayer ads was the illustration and copy. French artists, for starters. If you are going to borrow value for your product, begin with the best. Ayer went with Maillol and Derain, then later used Picasso, Matisse, and Edzard. The citation below the painting makes sure you know that this is a-r-t; it has a title, date, and easily viewed signature. Four-color was used almost from the start, not just to give the limited-edition art-book illusion, but also to make sure that the little stones in the lower margins would stand out big against a tinted background.

This is the same reason, incidentally, that diamonds are often displayed in store windows under little umbrellas: the shadows give the illusion of greater substance. And this explains as well the current "Shadows" TV campaign (from J. Walter Thompson; Ayer lost the account) in which the stones magically appear on the fingers of dark silhouettes. In the background we hear the surging strings of the "Shadows Theme" performed by the London Symphony Orchestra. So many people think that the music is classical that the Diamond Promotion Service now sells a tape for twelve dollars.

A generation ago the high-culture schmaltz was borrowed not from ersatz classical art and music, but from ladies-magazine poetry. The guys would look at the stones, they might glance at the artwork, but they would pass by the purple prose that women would read. This text is not really prose or poetry; it's treacle. Here are samples:

> How fair has been each precious moment of their plans come true ... their silent meeting at the altar steps, their first waltz at the gay reception, and now, these wondrous days together in a world that seems their very own. Each memory in turn is treasured in the lovely, lighted depths of her engagement diamond, to be an endless source of happy inspiration.

Or:

Each memory in turn is treasured in the lovely, lighted depths of her engagement diamond, to be an endless source of happy inspiration. For such a radiant role, her diamond need not be costly or of many carats, but it must be chosen with care.

Or:

There is only tomorrow for young couples newly engaged. Heedlessly they spend the present, flinging the days like golden coins along time's changing shore. And each, as it falls unseen, becomes a yesterday.

Where did they come up with this? In Educational Services Case History #8, published by *The Saturday Evening Post* as a service to young copywriters, the process is unfolded, at least as it related to the 1948–49 campaign. First the Creative/Production Board decided that the general idea for this campaign would be either springtime scenes from around the world or famous honeymoon spots. They gave the general idea to the copywriter who was supposed to spin the cotton candy. A copywriter explains:

In working this out I found that I was turning out copy with a poetic and emotional mood. It just seemed impossible to develop the springtime theme without getting poetic. In the honeymoon copy it was easier to get lighter, gayer and brighter copy. I talked this over with Plans and Art people and they agreed, so we decided among ourselves that the honeymoon theme would be the better one and to recommend that over the springtime theme [Educational Services 1948, 9].

In writing out the honeymoon copy, she would compose four longhand drafts, free-associating as she went along, trying to link the rock in with the ring in with the romantic mood. "This was something like working a crossword puzzle because my theme was the honeymoon and the problem was how to work in the subject of the engagement and thus have occasion to mention the ring" (Ibid.). Once she got the text, it went over to artwork where a suitable image was sketched, to be later commissioned.

I mention this process because it was from the exhaustion of writing such carbonated prose that the most compressed diamond of a headline was formed. In April of 1947, Frances Gerety was laboring mightily to get the puzzle of purple prose into the proper crossword boxes. She was exhausted from trying to come up with a new line that would bring together all the intrinsic and romantic qualities of the diamond and have it not make any sense whatsoever. As Gerety remembers it for Ayer's promotional literature, "Dog tired, I put my head down and said, 'Please God, send me a line.'" He must have because she wrote, "A Diamond Is Forever." Next morning she had brought forth "something good." And indeed she had.

Gerety's phrase precisely catches the synecdoche. This tiny diamond is forever, your huge love is forever, how can you even think you could pull them apart? The iron law of supply and demand turns to mush before these four words. More incredibly, the line works as powerfully in the twenty-nine languages into which it has been translated. Even the makers of James Bond films know that while the British Empire may crumble, *Diamonds Are Forever.*

What is amazing, of course, is that it's so patently untrue. The diamond may last forever, but you will die and so goes your undying love. Mortality cannot be revoked, even with great advertising. So that diamond *and* the love it signifies *must* stay in your family, testament to your immortal love. Someone must care for it. A stone becomes an heirloom.

If you read the copy of other ads in this series, you will often see the case subtly being made for "keeping it in the family." NEVER even think of selling your jewel: how unromantic, how sacrilegious.

And how wonderful for De Beers! They had made the purchase of their product essentially a one-decision act. Like the truly mystical blue-chip stock, the only question was when you bought it, not when you sold it. They had mopped up the aftermarket.

So when the male buys the diamond he memorializes this undying love. He throws away *Consumer Reports* and all their silly criteria, he follows his heart (or other glands), and puts his meddling mind to sleep. Remember, this act of love will last ... well, at least as long as a diamond. He buys this rock just before he enters the central rite of passage in Western culture. He buys it just before he becomes seriously sexual, just before parenthood, just before big-time responsibilities. He buys something totally worthless as a material, which he may not be able to afford, and which has no possible value to him in this next chapter of his life.

Nothing else in advertising history has compared with "A Diamond Is Forever" and the engagement ring. But, as befits a paradox so central to human existence, one can see that no culture can withstand it. In Japan, for instance, which had no elaborate wedding rituals other than the ancient Shinto rite of drinking rice wine from a wooden bowl and, in fact, even prohibited the importation of diamonds until 1959, the engagement ring is now worn by 80 percent of brides—about the same as in the United States.

Having learned the power of translating time worked into a testament of love, De Beers upped the ante. While the American male is told he should budget two months' salary, his Japanese

counterpart is told to devote three or four months' earnings to the purchase of his undying love symbol.

Although "nothing will bring back the hour of splendor in the grass," the cartel is eagerly trying to ritualize anniversaries. So, along with the tennis bracelet and ear studs, which eat up otherwise worthless supply from Australia and Siberia, we now have the "10th Diamond Anniversary Band" and the "25th Anniversary Diamond Necklace." Price? Simple, according to the ads. "How much do you love her after ten [or twenty-five] years of marriage?" Naturally, it's ten or twenty-five times as much. So you dig ten or twenty-five times as deep as the two-month-wages engagement ring.

Now, just for the fun of it, take those "brand-new gem stones" (already millions of years old) back to the store ten seconds after you have bought them, and see what they're worth. You'll be lucky to get 18 percent of what you just paid. But doing something sensible isn't the point, is it? If only it were, we'd be buying zirconium from the Home Shopping Network.

COKE AND CHRISTMAS

The Claus That Refreshes

TO MOVE YOUR PRODUCT out of the store, you first need to move it into the consumer's imagination. For, as social scientists have shown, it is hard to fight an enemy who has outposts in your mind. Very often this colonizing is done by positioning your object near some calendar event. The big hand strikes twelve and your object jumps out—like the clockwork cuckoo. You don't have to break through, you're already there.

The brass ring in advertising is, of course, to carry this off without detection. Some products have gotten themselves so deep inside the clock that they seem to have been there forever. Take the rhythms of passing through a day, for instance. Breakfast was a creation of the cereal companies (we used to eat dinner scraps to start the day), the coffee break used to be at four in the afternoon until the coffee roasters moved it away from tea time to the morning, the cocktail hour is an invention of the liquor industry, the Ploughman's Lunch was introduced to the English in the 1960s, not in the sixteenth century, and so forth.

As with a day, so with the year. Events like Super Bowl Sunday, the Oscars, Secretaries' Day, Spring Break, Cinco de Mayo, and even Saint Patrick's Day have been taken over by commercial interests. Anthropologists call the phenomenon by which one system is laid down over another *syncretism*. Advertisers call it nirvana.

Observe Halloween. Halloween started as just another pagan festival, this one having to do with the harvest and the coming of cold weather. Bonfires were lit and chants sung for safe passage

Coke's Santa by Haddon Sundblom for the *Things Go Better with Coke* campaign, 1964.

through dangerous winter. Bonfire Night was taken over by the Catholic Church to become All Hallow's Eve, with perhaps a little of Guy Fawkes' Day mixed in, accounting for the appearance of prankish games. All we now share with the Druids is the link with dying light, as this time marks our return to standard time and the end of daylight savings time. That we get dressed up in the costumes of characters that may well have scared us, that we demand and get treats, and that mischief is just below the surface, all reinforce Halloween as border ceremony between seasons and between childhood and adolescence.

For years this celebration was kept alive by candy makers. If you look carefully, sugar candy is at the heart of most consumption holidays. So we have candy hearts for Valentine's Day, chocolate eggs for Easter (no one bothers to ask what a rabbit is doing laying eggs), boxed candy for Mother's Day, candy corn for Thanksgiving, and striped candy canes for Christmas. The kings of candyland—Nestlé, Mars, and Hershey—have been able to "own" these holidays during which they sell special candy at full retail price. In fact, seasonal sugar accounts for most of these companies' profit, with Easter far in the lead with sales of more than half a billion dollars.

But the best advertising time-bomb by far is Coke's Santa Claus. You can keep Christ out of Christmas, but not Coke's Santa. This character, a weird conflation of Saint Nicholas (a down-on-his-luck nobleman who helped young ladies turn away from prostitution) and Kris Kringle (perhaps a German barbarism of "Christ-kintle," a gift giver), has become so powerful that when kids are told he doesn't exist, their parents become depressed.

Originally the image of Santa Claus was a creation of Clement Clarke Moore and Thomas Nast. In 1822, Moore wrote a poem for his daughters that was reprinted in newspapers and found its way a decade later into the *New York Book of Poetry*. In his poem, "The Visit From Saint Nicholas" (not "The Night Before Christmas"), an elflike creature runs about on Christmas Eve delivering presents. He is tiny, small enough to come down the chimney.

> *When what to my wondering eyes should appear,*
> *But a miniature sleigh, and eight tiny rein-deer;*
> *With a little old driver, so lively and quick,*
> *I knew in a moment it must be St. Nick.*

St. Nick was plumped up into a full-sized Santa by the editorial cartoonist Thomas Nast. In 1869 he collected his images from *Harper's Weekly* and published them in a book called *Santa Claus and His Works*. If we have Moore to thank for the reindeer (and all their great reindeer names), we have Nast to thank for fattening up Santa and sending him to the North Pole.

By the end of the nineteenth century, Santa was everywhere. He was in newspapers, in magazines, as a toy doll, on calendars, in children's books, and, thanks to the great chromolithographer Louis Prang, on Christmas cards. Owing to the innovation of the "chromo," he first appears in a multicolored suit sketched by Nast. Santa is not ready for prime time yet. He's too severe, too judgmental. He still needs a little tuck here, a little letting out there, he needs a big belt, a red coat, he needs those buccaneer boots, he needs a beard-trim—most of all, he needs to get warm and fuzzy.

The jolly old St. Nick that we know from countless images did not come from folklore, nor did he originate in the imaginations of Moore and Nast. He came from the yearly advertisements of the Coca-Cola Company. He wears the corporate colors—the famous red and white—for a reason: he is working out of Atlanta, not out of the North Pole. And while his polar bears may come from a Hollywood talent agency (CAA), his marketing comes from MBAs.

In the 1920s the Coca-Cola Company was having difficulty selling its soft drink during the winter. They wanted to make it a cold-weather beverage. "Thirst Knows No Season" was their initial winter campaign. At first they decided to show how a winter personage like Santa could enjoy a soft drink in December. They showed Santa chug-a-lugging with the Sprite Boy (the addled young soda jerk with the Coke bottle cap jauntily stuck on his head). But then they got lucky. They started showing Santa relaxing from his travails by drinking a Coke, then showed how the kids might leave a Coke (not milk) for Santa, and then implied that the gifts coming in from Santa were in exchange for the Coke. Paydirt. Perfect positioning! Santa's presents might not be in exchange for a Coke, but they were "worth" a Coke. Coke's Santa was elbowing aside other Santas. Coke's Santa was starting to "own" Christmas.

From the late 1930s until the mid-1950s, Haddon H. Sundblom had spent much of the year preparing his cuddly Santas for the D'Arcy Agency in St. Louis. First he painted a salesman friend, Lou Prentis from Muskegon, Michigan, and after Lou died, Sundblom went to the mirror and painted himself. Haddon was a big man and a big drinker. Mrs. Claus was based on Mrs. Sundblom.

Sundblom would do two or three Santas for mass-market magazines, especially *The Saturday Evening Post*, and then one for billboards, and maybe another for point-of-sale items. The paintings almost always showed Santa giving presents and receiving Coke, sharing his Coke with the kids surrounded by toys, playing with the toys and drinking the Coke, or reading a letter from a kid while drinking the Coke left like the glass of milk. The headlines read, "They Knew What I Wanted," "It's My Gift for Thirst," "And Now the Gift for Thirst," or "Travel Refreshed." He's a little mischievous, not above lifting a turkey leg from the fridge and sitting down a spell in Dad's comfy chair with the soon-to-be "traditional soft drink" of the season.

Sundblom was quick to glom on to any passing motif. After Disney made *Bambi,* a fawn was worked into the illustration, and after Gene Autry sang "Here Comes Santa Claus," a reindeer soon made his way into the happy scene. After all, the provenance of Rudolph the Red-Nosed Reindeer was pure commercialism. Rudolph was created by Robert L. May, a copywriter for Montgomery Ward, and his story proved so popular that 2.3 million copies of the musical score of "Rudolph" were sent out with the Ward catalog in 1939.

So complete was the colonization of Christmas that Coke's Santa had elbowed aside all comers by the 1940s. He was the Santa of the 1947 movie *Miracle on 34th Street* just as he is the Santa of the recent film *The Santa Clause*. He is the Santa on Hallmark cards, he is the Santa riding the Norelco shaver each Christmas season, he is the department-store Santa, and he is even the Salvation Army Santa!

Coca-Cola has been the happy beneficiary of this Darwinian struggle of images, and it has celebrated its success each December by putting Sundblom's creation on everything it owns. In fact, one of Coke's agencies, W. B. Doner & Co. (no relation to Donner, Blitzen, & Co.), is hired almost exclusively for the December hijinks. Sundblom's Santa is now on the corporation's Christmas cans of Coke Classic, is part of an art show that is trucked around from mall to mall each holiday season (even to the Louvre!), has his own Web site, is licensed to the Franklin Mint for a collector plate selling for $29.95, is on special Christmas tree decorations, and is star of a special television commercial in which he seems to come alive on one of the advertising panels of a delivery truck. The Sundblom Santa lifts his soft drink bottle in a holiday toast and winks.

As the horror films promise . . . he'll be coming around again. Keep watching the skies. Every Christmas, he'll be baaaack. Pity poor Pepsi. They must dread Christmas.

THE VOLKSWAGEN BEETLE

William Bernbach and the Fourth Wall

ONE OF THE MOST PROVOCATIVE ways to approach modern advertising is by considering individual ads in the context of what Harold Bloom has called "the anxiety of influence." Adapting the Freudian idea of Oedipal conflict, Bloom argued that any major poet must struggle for his own voice with a great predecessor whose strength both shapes and threatens to overcome the poetic "son." So Milton wrestled with Spenser, Keats with Shakespeare, and Wallace Stevens with Keats, Shelley, and Wordsworth. The poetic canon in English can thus be presented as an interfamilial struggle, with the successful "sons" breaking loose from the father and becoming "fathers" to the next generation, which must push past them. And so it goes.

What makes this mode of interpretation rewarding is that it can be applied to any creative family. So moviemakers like Quentin Tarantino are aware they are rewriting films of Hitchcock; architects are forever recasting the shapes; painters are retouching canvases; musicians are humming the tunes of others. The struggle is not just to be different; it is to be more powerful.

What makes advertising interesting in this regard is that the creative presence is usually anonymous (the copywriter does not sign his name, nor do we usually know what agency he works for), but his selling technique is out there for all to see. Again and again and again. As Howard Gossage, the iconoclastic paterfamilias of San Francisco advertising in the 1960s, once said sardonically, *Think Small*, 1962. "The object of your advertising should not be to communicate

Think small.

Our little car isn't so much of a novelty any more.

A couple of dozen college kids don't try to squeeze inside it.

The guy at the gas station doesn't ask where the gas goes.

Nobody even stares at our shape.

In fact, some people who drive our little flivver don't even think 32 miles to the gallon is going any great guns.

Or using five pints of oil instead of five quarts.

Or never needing anti-freeze.

Or racking up 40,000 miles on a set of tires.

That's because once you get used to some of our economies, you don't even think about them any more.

Except when you squeeze into a small parking spot. Or renew your small insurance. Or pay a small repair bill. Or trade in your old VW for a new one.

Think it over.

with your consumers and prospects at all, but to terrorize your competition's copywriters" (in Hampel 1988, 25).

From time to time the entire advertising industry changes as the result of a "strong" force elbowing others aside. Just as Chaucer, Milton, Shakespeare, and Wordsworth changed forever how we saw words in print, Claude Hopkins, David Ogilvy, and Rosser Reeves changed the face of modern advertising. After them, the endeavor never looked the same. And in changing the surface, they changed the way we looked at, and talked about, the manufactured world of machine-made things.

The "strong" artist, however, is never simply imitative or derivative; he is always radical. As Gossage says, he "terrorizes." Very often his terror appears as a kind of hauteur, a self-conscious, even aggressive, desire not just to denigrate what has come before, but to render it old-fashioned. When he is successful, he upsets not only his colleagues but also his clients. He changes the way *they* look at what they manufacture.

William Bernbach was such a strong force in American advertising for a number of reasons. First, he was one of a handful of Jews in a sea of Protestants. When he entered advertising in the 1940s, the agency world was not dissimilar to that world portrayed by Frederic Wakeman in the best-selling novel *The Hucksters* (1946). The client called the shots, and the agency, staffed by sycophants from Scarsdale, carried out his wishes. For their docility they pocketed the standard 15-percent commission and had ulcers.

Agency life at mid-century was all very white-shoe and gray-flannel-suit. Jews—ironically, perhaps because of their heritage as merchandisers—were disparaged.

So it is especially ironic that the "Jewish agency" was called Grey Advertising, and it was here that Bernbach worked from 1945 to 1949. He rose rapidly to vice-president in charge of art and copy. He worked closely with Mr. Doyle, the vice-president and account supervisor. On June 1, 1949, they and Mr. Dane, who had been running a small advertising agency on his own, established Doyle Dane Bernbach Inc. No commas separated the names because the partners pledged that nothing would come between them—not even punctuation.

Perhaps you can see even in this corporate title a sense of what will characterize DDB advertising: it is us against them. Brown shoes and gabardine.

Many of DDB's clients were Jewish, and they made no attempt to disguise it. They came up from the street, not down from the hill, from NYU, not Princeton. In fact, they flaunted grit. Outré became classé, which was no mean trick in a world still riddled with anti-Semitism.

So for Orbach's, a Manhattan clothing outlet, they advertised "high fashion at low prices" with copy lifted from the catty patois of the Catskills: "The way she talks, you'd think she was in *Who's Who*. Well! I found out what's with *her*.... I just happened to be going her way and *I saw Joan come out of Orbach's!*" For Levy's bread, they boldfaced the headline "You don't have to be Jewish to love Levy's" over the smiling faces of everyone but Jews. And for El Al, the national airline of Israel, they featured a Jewish mother talking about "my son, the pilot," a send-up of "my son, the doctor," and started with such leads as "We don't take off until everything is kosher."

So what's a nice little Jewish agency doing with a client like Volkswagen, a car designed by Ferdinand Porsche in 1938 to be "the people's car" and fostered by Hitler (and we know how he felt about all those people not "his" people)?

No one knows why DDB took on VW, but I suspect the taint was part of the attraction. All his life, Bernbach kept mum on this volatile political subject. His work did the speaking. In his posthumous memoir, compiled by Bob Levenson, a life-long colleague, but titled *Bill Bernbach's Book: A History of the Advertising That*

Changed the History of Advertising, we are told twice in the 400-word introduction to the VW section that Bernbach's mantra was always "The product. The product. Stay with the product."

If these Jewish guys could sell *that* German product, it would be like the young cub outdoing the old master. Do that and you clear out a space for yourself in the pantheon of greats. You become, in Bloom's terms, a "strong" artist. Your influence makes others anxious. As Jerry Della Femina was to say years later, "In the beginning, there was Volkswagen. That's the first campaign which everyone can trace back and say, 'This is where the changeover began'" (Della Femina 1970, 28). Here is the opening volley of the Creative Revolution.

In many ways Bernbach was perfectly fitted to Volkswagen. They were both at the margin of the world around them, on the edge. Years after Bernbach's death, a colleague reminisced in the trade journal *Advertising Age*:

> To understand what made Bill tick you need to know how much he hated imperfection. Any imperfection. He couldn't rest until he had fixed it. He hated the imperfection of being short and pudgy. He hated being Jewish—not because he felt ethnically defensive, but because it was parochial. He told me once that when he was five years old he saw a little blond girl. He fell instantly in love and vowed that when he grew up he would marry a Christian. Which he did. At the time I first met him he was unsophisticated and ill at ease. Out of his depth socially. This really bothered him. When he was with the World's Fair he traveled to Washington with his boss, who gave him a roll of quarters and taught him how to tip. In the beginning his clothes looked scruffy. The dress sense came later with success. He was infinitely painstaking about his appearance—it had to be perfect, just like his ads. He wouldn't wear white shirts, only blue ones, because white accented his paleness. He fussed over every detail in the same way that he

spent hours ... cutting up repro proofs and sliding them around until they fit exactly. He told me that his son, Paul, always said he was the only man alive who could spend an hour dressing in the bathroom and come out looking exactly like yesterday [Hixon 1986, 24].

I mention this anxious sense of self because, just as surely as you can see the painter in the pentimento, you can see Bernbach re-created in the personality of his Volkswagen ads. When critics talk about Bernbach's contribution to advertising, they invariably mention that he gave personality to products. Think only of "The Chivas Regal of Scotches"; Mobil's "We want you to live"; Sony's "Tummy Television"; Avis's "We try harder"; Mikey; Juan Valdez; the American Tourister "Gorilla"; the Alka-Seltzer campaigns; and, of course, "You don't have to be Jewish to love Levy's."

The reason why the Volkswagen personality was so well defined, I think, is that it was Bernbach's own. It was Bernbach on wheels. The Beetle was not a German car—that was the Mercedes-Benz. It was a Jewish car! Look at the entire campaign from the first full-page black-and-white ad under the headline "Is Volkswagen contemplating a change?" to the last in 1978 of the VW logo dropping a tear under "Going, going ...," and you will see a remarkable coherence. The car never steps out of character.

That character is a wily combination of the *schlemiel* (the bumbler) and the *mensch* (the good heart). The car is cast as the Yiddish "little man," the self-effacing worrier, the guy who is always trying to get it right. This character has been a staple of filmic folklore from Buster Keaton and Charlie Chaplin to Woody Allen. He is the odd man out, the strange man in a stranger world. But under the self-conscious and anxious klutz is the caring and conscientious friend who will not desert you in times of need. Okay, he may not get the girl, but that's only because she's not smart enough.

The Magic Touch of Tomorrow!

The *look* of success! The *feel* of success! The *power* of success!
They come to you in a dramatically beautiful, dynamically powered
new Dodge that introduces the ease and safety of push-button driving
—the Magic Touch of Tomorrow! It is a truly great value.

New '56 DODGE
VALUE LEADER OF THE FORWARD LOOK

**The Magic
of Tomorrow:
the 1956 Dodge,
1955.**

The challenge to make the little man attractive was redoubled by the fact that when DDB got the VW account, American cars and their advertising were going over the top into the world of macho superheroes. Cars were becoming screaming jet planes. Not only were they sprouting massive tail fins, presumably to stabilize their otherwise out-of-control horsepower, but models were being named B-58 (Buick) or F-85 (Oldsmobile) in honor of their air force cousins. A 1958 Dodge advertisement invited readers to "take off" in their new model that had the "new Swept-Wing look for 1959 . . . set off by thrusting Jet-Trail Tail Lamps." The 1958 Buick labored under forty-four pounds of streamlined chrome to make this point.

As Detroit was bloating toward self-parody, Bernbach, his chief VW copywriter, Julian Koenig, and art director Helmut Krone were standing by. The little man would throw sand at the helplessly overmuscled Charles Atlas.

Maybe they had no choice. The truth about the People's Car was that it was small, ugly, non-obsolescent, and foreign. Maybe all DDB did was make a virtue out of necessity. But it was the way they did it that changed forever the nature of advertising. Objects have always had sexes (language shows us that); from here on they would have personalities.

"Think Small," for example. First, the obvious. *Cherchez la femme.* Where's the girl? Since men were the primary purchasers of automobiles, ads of mid-century invariably featured a winsome female. The code was not hard to crack. It was the same code that informed the selling of beer or aftershave: buy the product, get the girl.

Next, where's the car? It is hard to find. The more standard way to showcase curvaceous pig iron is to put it at the end of your nose. This was accomplished in any number of ways, most commonly by not photographing the car but by illustrating it large against an exciting backdrop. Often we look down the fin or hood to the complementary sex object who is just barely touching it.

What we get in this ad, however, is vast amounts of blank space with just a postage stamp of a car. We have to work to see it. In fact, we have to work to consume this new kind of advertising. Ask anyone who grew up during the 1950s to conjugate *amo, amas, amat*, ask them to do their multiplication tables, ask them a few state capitals, and you can see what work at an early age will do for memory. Ask them to remember Volkswagen ads, and you will be amazed by the recall. They know them. They know the ad with the headline "Lemon," the VW shape over graph paper, the floating car, the egg car, the "'51, '52, '53, '54 … Volkswagen" under the same picture, the tire tracks in snow, "ugly is only skin-deep." They know them because you had to study these ads. Unlike other ads of the time, they were not billboards passing at warp speed. These were like homework assignments; you had to spend time with them.

And when you read them, they didn't behave like advertising copy. First, where is the fancy serif typeface and gaudy color? How come the paragraphs are in half-lines, not in text blocks? Isn't there a lot of blank space? Why is the company talking to us in hushed tones, and why is the appeal to the brain, not the glands?

And, most important, why are they making a fetish of truth-in-the-negative? "Our car isn't this" and "our car isn't that." It's not big, it's not fast, it's not beautiful, it's not … and then, suddenly, halfway through, the negatives turn positive. Our car doesn't eat gas, oil, and tires. It doesn't need antifreeze, a big parking spot, and high insurance premiums.

In the midst of this invocation of negatives becoming positives comes the anachronism "flivver." Flivver is certainly not part of adspeak. The prolepsis, as it is known in rhetoric, works because the VW simply cannot be analogized to any monsters now slouching from Detroit. Instead, it is reminiscent of the way cars used to be (or at least how we may romanticize them): honest, durable, thrifty, practical, cheap—the indomitable Model T, the car, as Henry Ford said, for The Great Multitude. Well, as IBM was saying at almost the same time, *Think* it over.

That having been said, one should quickly add, *think* but don't think too hard. For although the appeal to truth is made, it is not being made to the whole truth. Had it done so, we would have been informed that there was little head and shoulder room in the backseat, that the engine lasted about 50,000 miles, that it was slow and noisy, and that this was not the car to be in if you were in a head-on or a side-impact crash.

What is happening here in the VW ads is the effacement of the fourth wall in advertising. Just as playwrights like Bertolt Brecht and novelists like John Barth were opening up the form and letting the reader into the action, so, too, William Bernbach was attempting the same feat. You were not being lectured, you were being included.

By the 1970s the deed was almost done. In a 1969 television commercial called "1949 Auto Show," you can see how far things had come. Joe Isuzu is right around the corner. This spot starts with an old-time announcer stepping up to the microphone and intoning, "And now the star of the 1949 Auto Show. The car the public wants. The all-new DeSoto." The camera pans to another exhibit, presided over by a white-coated scientist who is extolling the air-induction ports of a Detroit behemoth. Pan left: another adman is rhapsodizing over a Packard. Fourth scene: the Adams sisters harmonizing "Longer, lower, wider … the '49 Hudson is the car for you." Last scene: over in the corner, unnoticed by the milling throngs, is a bow-tied solitary soul, the little man personified. Here's what he says: "So Volkswagen will constantly be changing, improving, and refining their car. Not necessarily to keep in style with the times, but to make a better car. Which means, to all of you, better mileage." The camera pulls back to the voice-over, "Of all the promises made at the 1949 Auto Show, we at Volkswagen kept ours."

VW "1949 Auto Show"

1 And now the star of the 1949 Auto Show. The car of the future. The car the public wants. The all-new De Soto!

2 So there's no doubt about it. Next year every car in America will have holes in its side.

3 So the man to see if you're buying your next car for keeps is your nearby Packard dealer!

4 (singing) Longer, lower, wider … The '49 Hudson is the car for you!

5 So Volkswagen will constantly be changing, improving, and refining their car. Not necessarily to keep in style with the times, but to make a better car. Which means, to all of you, better mileage.

6 (VO) Of all the promises made at the 1949 Auto Show, we at Volkswagen kept ours.

The 1949 Auto Show, 1969.

This tradition of co-opting cool still continues. In fact, letting the audience in on the secret, opening the fourth wall, has become the default mode of establishing rapport in much modern advertising. But long before Generation X ever thought of subverting commercialism by pretending to be outside its influence, Bernbach was already there. In this sense, he is indeed the legitimate heir to Barnum. Just as the Prince of Humbug had used his audiences' skepticism as a lever to open doors, so too did Bernbach use the products' shortcomings as a lever to close the sale. Both men knew the power of irony is that what is withheld is often far more alluring than what is put forward. Here, they say to us with a smile, just take a little peek behind the curtain. Have a look at the Wizard of Oz. And we do.

11

MISS CLAIROL'S "DOES SHE . . . OR DOESN'T SHE?"

How to Advertise a Dangerous Product

TWO TYPES OF PRODUCTS are difficult to advertise: the very common and the very radical. Common products, called "parity products," need contrived distinctions to set them apart. You announce them as "New and Improved, Bigger and Better." But singular products need the illusion of acceptability. They have to appear as if they were *not* new and big, but old and small.

So, in the 1950s, new objects like television sets were designed to look like furniture so that they would look "at home" in your living room. Meanwhile, accepted objects like automobiles were growing massive tail fins to make them seem bigger and better, new and improved.

Although hair coloring is now very common (about half of all American women between the ages of thirteen and seventy color their hair, and about one in eight American males between thirteen and seventy does the same), such was certainly not the case generations ago. The only women who regularly dyed their hair were actresses like Jean Harlow, and "fast women," most especially prostitutes. The only man who dyed his hair was Gorgeous George, the professional wrestler. He was also the only man to use perfume.

In the twentieth century, prostitutes have had a central role in developing cosmetics. For them, sexiness is an occupational necessity, and hence anything that makes them look young, flushed, and fertile is quickly assimilated. Creating a full-lipped, big-eyed, and rosy-cheeked image is the basis of the lipstick, eye shadow, mascara, and rouge industries. While fashion may come

Does She . . . or Doesn't She?: Miss Clairol in 1955.

Does she...or doesn't she?

Hair color so natural only her hairdresser knows for sure!

She's as full of fun as a kid—and just as fresh looking! Her hair sparkles with clear, radiant, young color that looks as natural in the bright light of snow as it does in the soft light of a candle. And *this* is the beautiful difference with Miss Clairol. In *every* light, Miss Clairol hair color looks natural. It keeps your hair lovely to touch—silky, shiny, in wonderful condition.

Hairdressers everywhere prefer Miss Clairol to all other haircolorings, recommend it, use it every time to freshen fading color. Its *automatic color timing* is most dependable. And Miss Clairol really covers gray. But best of all, they love the lively, natural look of it, the soft, ladylike tone. And so will you. So try Miss Clairol yourself. Today. Creme Formula or Regular.

MISS CLAIROL HAIR COLOR BATH

THE NATURAL-LOOKING HAIRCOLORING ● MORE WOMEN USE MISS CLAIROL THAN ALL OTHER HAIRCOLORING COMBINED *down* from the couturiers, face paint comes *up* from the street. Yesterday's painted woman is today's fashion plate.

In the 1950s, just as Betty Friedan was sitting down to write *The Feminine Mystique*, there were three things a lady should not do. She should not smoke in public, she should not wear long pants (unless under an overcoat), and she should not color her hair. Better she should pull out each gray strand by its root than risk association with those who bleached or, worse, dyed their hair.

This was the cultural context into which Lawrence M. Gelb, a chemical broker and enthusiastic entrepreneur, presented his product to Foote, Cone & Belding. Gelb had purchased the rights to a French hair coloring process called Clairol. The process was unique in that unlike other available hair-coloring products, which coated the hair, Clairol actually penetrated the hair shaft, producing softer, more natural tones. Moreover, it contained a foamy shampoo base and mild oils that cleaned and conditioned the hair.

When the product was first introduced during World War II, the application process took five different steps and lasted a few hours. The users were urban and wealthy. In 1950, after seven years of research and development, Gelb once again took the beauty industry by storm. He introduced the new Miss Clairol Hair Color Bath, a single-step hair-coloring process.

This product, unlike any haircolor previously available, lightened, darkened, or changed a woman's natural haircolor by coloring and shampooing hair in one simple step that took only twenty minutes. Color results were more natural than anything you could find at the corner beauty parlor. It was hard to believe. Miss Clairol was so technologically advanced that demonstrations had to be done onstage at the International Beauty Show, using buckets of water, to prove to the industry that it was not a hoax. This breakthrough was almost too revolutionary to sell.

In fact, within six months of Miss Clairol's introduction, the number of women who visited the salon for permanent haircoloring services increased by more than 500 percent! The women still didn't think they could do it themselves. And *Good House-keeping* magazine rejected hair-color advertising because they too didn't believe the product would work. The magazine waited for three years before finally reversing its decision, accepting the ads, and awarding Miss Clairol's new product the "Good Housekeeping Seal of Approval."

FC&B passed the "Yes you *can* do it at home" assignment to Shirley Polykoff, a zesty and genial first-generation American in her late twenties. She was, as she herself was the first to admit, a little unsophisticated, but her colleagues thought she understood how women would respond to abrupt change. Polykoff understood emotion, all right, and she also knew that you could be outrageous if you did it in the right context. You can be very naughty if you are first perceived as being nice. Or, in her words, "Think it out square, say it with flair." And it is just this reconciliation of opposites that informs her most famous ad.

She knew this almost from the start. On July 9, 1955, Polykoff wrote to the head art director that she had three campaigns for Miss Clairol Hair Color Bath. The first shows the same model in each ad, but with slightly different hair color. The second exhorts "Tear up those baby pictures! You're a redhead now," and plays on the American desire to refashion the self by rewriting history. These two ideas were, as she says, "knock-downs" en route to what she really wanted. In her autobiography, appropriately titled *Does She ... Or Doesn't She?: And How She Did It*, Polykoff explains the third execution, the one that will work:

> #3. Now here's the one I really want. If I can get it sold to the client. Listen to this: *"Does she ... or doesn't she?"* (No, I'm not kidding. Didn't you ever hear of the arresting question?) Followed by: *"Only her mother knows for sure!"* or *"So natural, only her mother knows for sure!"*

I may not do the mother part, though as far as I'm concerned mother is the ultimate authority. However, if Clairol goes
retail, they may have a problem of offending beauty salons,
where they are presently doing all of their business. So I may
change the word "mother" to "hairdresser." This could be awfully
good business—turning the hairdresser into a color expert.
Besides, it reinforces the claim of naturalness, and not so incidentally, glamorizes the salon.

The psychology is obvious. I know from myself. If anyone
admires my hair, I'd rather die than admit I dye. And since I feel
so strongly that the average woman is me, this great stress on
naturalness is important [Polykoff 1975, 28–29].

While her headline is naughty, the picture is nice and natural.
Exactly what "Does She…or Doesn't She" do? To men the answer
was clearly sexual, but to women it certainly was not. The male
editors of *Life* magazine balked about running this headline until
they did a survey and found out women were not filling in the
ellipsis the way they were.

Women, as Polykoff knew, were finding different meaning
because they were actually looking at the model and her child. For
them the picture was not presexual but postsexual, not inviting
male attention but expressing satisfaction with the result. Miss
Clairol is a mother, not a love interest.

If that is so, then the product must be misnamed: it should be
Mrs. Clairol. Remember, this was the mid-1950s, when illegiti-
macy was a powerful taboo. Out-of-wedlock children were still
called bastards, not love children. This ad was far more dangerous
than anything Benetton or Calvin Klein has ever imagined.

The naughty/nice conundrum was further intensified *and* dif-
fused by some of the ads featuring a wedding ring on the model's
left hand. Although FC&B experimented with models purporting

to be secretaries, schoolteachers, and the like, the motif of mother and child was always constant.

So what was the answer to what she does or doesn't do? To women, what she did had to do with visiting the hairdresser. Of course, men couldn't understand. This was the world before unisex hair care. Men still went to barber shops. This was the same pre-feminist generation in which the solitary headline "Modess... because" worked magic selling female sanitary products. The ellipsis masked a knowing implication that excluded men. That was part of its attraction. Women know, men don't. This you-just-don't-get-it

A Miss Clairol retrospective from *Life* magazine, 1963.

motif was to become a central marketing strategy as the women's movement was aided *and* exploited by Madison Avenue niche-meisters.

Polykoff had to be ambiguous for another reason. As she notes in her memo, Clairol did not want to be obvious about what they were doing to their primary customer—the beauty shop. Remember that the initial product entailed five different steps performed by the hairdresser, and lasted hours. Many women were still using hairdressers for something they could now do by themselves. It did not take a detective to see that the company was trying to run around the beauty shop and sell to the end-user. So the ad again has it both ways. The hairdresser is invoked as the expert—only he knows *for sure*—but the process of coloring your hair can be done without his expensive assistance.

The copy block on the left of the finished ad (see page 119) reasserts this intimacy, only now it is not the hairdresser speaking, but another woman who has used the product. The emphasis is always on *returning* to young and radiant hair, hair you used to have, hair, in fact, that glistens exactly like your current companion's—your child's hair.

The copy block on the right is all business and was never changed during the campaign. The process of coloring is always referred to as "automatic color tinting." *Automatic* was to the fifties what *plastic* became to the sixties, and what *networking* is today. Just as your food was kept automatically fresh in the refrigerator, your car had an automatic transmission, your house had an automatic thermostat, your dishes and clothes were automatically cleaned and dried, so, too, your hair had automatic tinting.

However, what is really automatic about hair coloring is that once you start, you won't stop. Hair grows, roots show, buy more product … automatically. The genius of Gillette was not just that they sold the "safety razor" (they could give the razor away), but that they also sold the concept of being *clean-shaven*. Clean-shaven means that you use their blade every day, so, of course, you always need more blades. Clairol made "roots showing" into what Gillette had made "five o'clock shadow."

As was to become typical in hair coloring ads, the age of the model was a good ten years younger than the typical product user. The model is in her early thirties (witness the age of the child), too young to have gray hair.

This aspirational motif was picked up later for other Clairol products: "If I've only one life … let me live it as a blonde!" "Every woman should be a redhead … at least once in her life!" "What would your husband say if suddenly you looked 10 years younger?" "Is it true blondes have more fun?" "What does he look at second?" And, of course, "The closer he gets the better you look!"

But these slogans for different brand extensions only work

because Miss Clairol had done her job. She made hair coloring possible, she made hair coloring acceptable, she made at-home hair coloring—dare I say it—empowering. She made the unique into the commonplace. By the 1980s, the hairdresser problem had been long forgotten and the follow-up lines read, "Hair color so natural, they'll never know for sure."

The Clairol theme propelled sales 413 percent higher in six years and influenced nearly 50 percent of all adult women to tint their tresses. Ironically, Miss Clairol, bought out by Bristol-Myers in 1959, also politely opened the door to her competitors, L'Oreal and Revlon.

Thanks to Clairol, hair coloring has become a very attractive business indeed. The key ingredients are just a few pennies' worth of peroxide, ammonia, and pigment. In a pretty package at the drugstore it sells for four to ten dollars per application. To put it mildly, the cost-revenue spread is what is really enticing. Gross profits of 70 percent are standard. As is common in the beauty industry, advertising and promotion cost far more than the product.

If you want to see how well this Clairol campaign did, just look at how L'Oreal sells its version of hair dye. In L'Oreal's pitch, a rapturous beauty proudly proclaims that her coloring costs more, but that "I'm worth it." In a generation, hair coloring has gone from a surreptitious whisper (Does she...?) to a heroic trumpet (You better believe I do!). The user may be dangerous, the product certainly isn't. L'Oreal now dominates the worldwide market.

But by taking control of how the new woman presented herself, Miss Clairol did indeed make it possible to come a long way, baby. In a current ad for Miss Clairol's descendant Nice 'n' Easy, the pixieish Julia Louis-Dreyfus, from *Seinfeld,* shows us how the unique and dangerous has become common and tame. In her Elaine persona, she interrupts a wedding, telling the bride, "Even if your marriage doesn't last, your haircolor will." The guests are not shocked; they nod understandingly.

THE MARLBORO MAN

The Perfect Campaign

ALTHOUGH ADVERTISING AGENCIES love giving themselves prizes, there has been no award for the perfect campaign. If there were, Marlboro would win. Suffice it to say that this brand went from selling less than one quarter of one percent of the American market in the early 1950s to being the most popular in the entire world in just twenty years. Every fourth cigarette smoked is a Marlboro. Leo Burnett's brilliant campaign made Marlboro the most valuable brand in the world.

First, let's dispense with the politics of the product. We all know that cigarettes are the most dangerous legal product in the world. They kill more people each year than do guns. And yes, it is dreadful that the myth of independence is used to sell addiction. But never forget as well that it is exactly this danger that animates the Marlboro Man. He came into being just as smoking became problematic and, ironically, as long as anxiety exists, so will he.

And, second, cigarettes, like domestic beer and bottled water, build deep affiliations that have absolutely nothing to do with taste. As David Ogilvy said, "Give people a taste of Old Crow and *tell* them it's Old Crow. Then give them another taste of Old Crow, *but tell them it's Jack Daniel's*. Ask them which they prefer. They'll think the two drinks are quite different. *They are tasting images*" (Ogilvy 1985, 87).

In fact, it was the cigarette companies that found this out first. In the 1920s they blindfolded brand-dedicated smokers and put them into dark rooms. Then they gave them Luckies, Pall Malls, Chesterfields, and Camels, as well as European smokes, and asked

The Marlboro Man in the 1950s.

The filter doesn't get between you and the flavor!

Marlboro

THE NEW FILTER CIGARETTE FROM PHILIP MORRIS

NEW FLIP-TOP BOX

Firm to keep cigarettes from crushing. No tobacco in your pocket.

Marlboro
LONG SIZE

POPULAR FILTER PRICE

Yes, this easy-drawing but hard-working filter sure delivers the goods on flavor. Popular filter price. This new Marlboro makes it easy to change to a filter. This one you'll like.

(MADE IN RICHMOND, VIRGINIA, FROM A NEW PHILIP MORRIS RECIPE) the smokers to identify "their own brand"—the one they were sure they knew. By now we all know the results. Taste has basically little or nothing to do with why people choose specific brands of cigarettes.

Just as we drink the label, we smoke the advertising. So what's so smokable, so tasty, about this ad?

First, everything fits around the dominant image. The heading and the logotype fall naturally in place. Product name mediates between visual and verbal. Let's start with the name, *Marlboro*. Like so many cigarette brand names, it is English and elegant and, like its counterpart Winston, deceptively vague. Like the joke about how there's gotta be a pony in there somewhere, there's gotta be prestige in here somewhere. (Oddly enough, Marlboro was first created in Victorian England, then transported to the States as a cigarette for women.) The ersatz PM crest at the apex of the "red roof" chevron on the package hints of a bloodline, and the Latin motto "Veni, Vidi, Vici" (!) conveys ancient warrior strength. Clearly, the power is now both in the pack and in the buckaroo.

The buckaroo is, of course, the eponymous Marlboro Man. He is what we have for royalty, distilled manhood. (Alas, the Winston man barely exists. What little of him there is is opinionated, urbane, self-assured—and needs to tell you so.) The Marlboro Man needs to tell you nothing. He carries no scepter, no gun. He never even speaks. Doesn't need to. The difference between Marlboro and Winston is the difference between myth and reality. Winston needed to break the rules publicly to be independent ("Winston tastes good *like* a cigarette should"), the Marlboro Man has already been there, done that. Little wonder the Viceroy man ("a thinking man's filter, a smoking man's taste") couldn't even make the cut.

Generating prestige *and* independence is a crucial aspect of cigarette selling. If you are targeting those who are just entering the consumption community, and if the act of consumption is dangerous, then you do not need to stress rebellion—that's a given. What you need to announce is initiation into the pack.

When R.J. Reynolds tested Marlboro on focus groups, they found that it was not rugged machismo that was alluring to young Marlboro smokers, but separation from restraints (the tattoo) *and* a sense of belonging (Marlboro Country). This "secret" RJR report, now available on the World Wide Web, is one reason why the "I'd walk a mile for a Camel" man was subsumed into the more personable, intelligent, and independent "Cool Joe" Camel.

Let's face it, the Camel man was downright stupid. In the most repeated of his ill-fated "walk a mile" ads he is shown carrying a tire (instead of rolling it) across the desert (with no canteen), wearing no shade-providing hat. That he seemingly forgot the spare tire is as stupid as his choosing to smoke. Little wonder Cool Joe pushed him aside. A camel seems intelligent in comparison.

The Marlboro Man's transformation was less traumatic, but no less meaningful. In fact, it is a reversal of the most popular tabloid story of the 1950s. It was to be, as David Ogilvy would say, one of the "riskiest decisions ever made" and one "which few advertisers would take." Here's the cultural context on a thumbnail, and what Philip Morris did about it:

On February 13, 1953, George Jorgenson went to Denmark and returned as Christine. The idea that one could change one's sex was profoundly unsettling to American culture. Once back at home, she uttered the perhaps apocryphal testament to his journey: "Men are wary of me and I'm wary of the ones who aren't."

At almost the same time, another repositioning was occurring. Now, as any modern ten-year-old can tell you, objects have sexual characteristics, too. Philip Morris had a female cigarette, Marlboro, that wouldn't sell. So they sent her up to Chicago to be re-gendered by Leo Burnett. Miss Marlboro was a "sissy smoke ... a tea room smoke," Burnett said. Although she had been in and out

The Marlboro woman of the 1940s.

of production for most of the century, in her most recent incarnation she had a red filter tip (called the "beauty tip," to hide lipstick stains) and a long-running theme: "Mild as May." Men wouldn't touch her, nor would many women.

In December 1954, Burnett took Miss Marlboro out to his gentleman's farm south of Chicago and invited some of his agency cohorts over to brainstorm. Something had to be done to put some hair on her chest, to change her out of pinafores and into cowboy chaps, anything to get her out of the suffocating tea room.

"What is the most masculine figure in America?" Burnett asked. "Cab driver, sailor, marine, pilot, race car driver" came the replies. Then someone simply said, "Cowboy." Bingo! Copywriter Draper Daniels filled in the blank: this smoke "Delivers the Goods on Flavor."

But these admen were not thinking of a real cowboy, not some dirty, spitting, toothless, smelly wrangler. They were city boys who knew cowboys in bronzes and oils by Frederic Remington, or in oils and watercolors by Charles Russell, or in the purple prose of Owen Wister's *The Virginian* or in the pulp of Zane Grey's countless novels. Philip Morris and Leo Burnett now love to tell you that the Marlboro Man was always a "real cowboy." Just don't remind them that almost half of the real cowpunchers were black or Mexican.

No matter, Leo Burnett had just the image in mind. He remembered seeing one C. H. Long, a thirty-nine-year-old foreman at the JA Ranch in the Texas panhandle, a place described as "320,000 acres of nothing much," who had been heroically photographed by Leonard McCombe for a cover of *Life* magazine in 1949. In other words, this Marlboro cowboy was a real/reel cowboy, something like what Matt Dillon, played by James Arness, was on television. A slightly roughed-up, *High Noon* Gary Cooper, a lite-spaghetti Clint Eastwood.

To get to this image, the Leo Burnett Company tried out all manner of windblown wranglers, some professional models, some not. Then, in 1963, just as the health concerns about lung cancer really took hold, they discovered Carl "Big-un" Bradley at the 6666 Ranch in Guthrie, Texas. Carl was the first real cowboy they used, and from then on the Marlboro Men were honest-to-God cowboys, rodeo riders, and stuntmen.

One look at him and you know: no Ralph Lauren jeans, no 401(k) plans, no wine spritzers, nothing with little ducks all over it, just independence, pure and simple. He doesn't concern himself with the Surgeon General. He's his own sheriff. To make sure he stayed that way, all background was airbrushed out. Later he got a grubstake in Marlboro Country.

Even today the Philip Morris Company receives letters from all over the world, mostly at the beginning of the summer, from travelers wishing to know how to get to Marlboro Country.

But there's more to the ad than the free-ranging cowboy. That package with the insignia, built truck-tough as a flip-top *box*, was a badge. With its hearty red, white, and black lettering, the smoker pinned it to his chest on the average of twenty-three times a day. This *vade mecum* of a package was designed by Frank Gianninoto and carefully tested through consumer surveys by Elmo

Roper & Associates and the Color Research Institute. Now the *Veni, Vidi, Vici* starts making sense. With this package you are the decorated conqueror. You burn bridges, bust broncos, confront stuff like lung cancer.

Sure, the girlie filter was there for the women (incidentally, the famous Marlboro red came from the lipstick red of the original "beauty filter"), but it was battled by the box, the medallion—the manliness of it all.

Should you still not be convinced, there was always the brand, the literal brand—the tattoo. Remember, this was the 1950s, when tattoos were not a fashion accessory, but an unambiguous sign of antisocial "otherness." But this brand was not on the biceps to signify Charles Atlas manliness; rather it was on the back of the smoking hand, or on the wrist. A strange place for a tattoo, to be sure, but appropriate.

Although research departments may cringe to hear this, the tattoo was not the result of motivational research showing that the image would be super macho. Leo Burnett supposedly thought the tattoo would "say to many men that here is a successful man who used to work with his hands," while "to many women, we believe it will suggest a romantic past."

But there is another story that also may be true. Alas, it doesn't emphasize virility and romance but the bugaboo of interpretation, namely, happenstance. It seems someone at the agency had scribbled on the hand of the *Life* magazine cowboy that there was no copyright clearance for this particular image. The agency sent this image in a paste-up to Philip Morris and then made another version from another cowboy photo to avoid copyright problems. It, too, went to the client. Back came the reaction: "Where's the tattoo on the second cowboy?" Perplexed agency people dug up the original photo and saw the warning scribbled across the wrist (McGuire 1989, 23).

No matter what the story, the tattoo stuck, not because of any massive testing but because everyone knew the branding itself was compelling. You are what you smoke.

When a campaign "works," every part seems compelling. In fact, in great ads, as in great works of art, the sum of the parts is always more than the whole. The visual and verbal rhetoric is so strong that they seem to have always been in place. They seem indestructible. In truth, however, often the greatest act of creativity is knowing when to leave well enough alone. "I have learned that any fool can write a bad ad," Burnett says in one of his pithy *100 Leo's*, "but that it takes a real genius to keep his hands off a good one" (Burnett 1995, 53).

Most of the tinkering with this campaign has been by the government. For instance, many people thought that by removing the Marlboro Man from television in the early 1970s the feds would send him into the sunset. No such luck. You can take down all the billboards and remove him from magazines. "Just a little dab" of this rhetoric "will do ya."

When Philip Morris attempted to introduce brand extension —Marlboro Light—after all the advertising bans were in place, all they did was unsaddle the cowboy and foreground the horse. Now that even mentioning the cigarette by name is becoming taboo, they are mining the original campaign by making Marlboro Country into Marlboro Unlimited and selling lots of logo'd stuff to smokers, calling it Gear Without Limits. By selling annually some 20 million T-shirts, caps, jackets, and other items bearing Marlboro logos, Philip Morris was, for a time, the nation's third-largest mail-order house.

This attempt to get around the fear of legal restrictions on advertising is called "sell-through," and you see it happening with almost all the major cigarette and beer brands. So Smokin' Joe, the super-cool Camel musician, appears on a host of nontobacco products like clothing, beach towels, baseball caps, while at the same time he also appears on the hit list of the FTC as a public nuisance.

And so what is Gear Without Limits for people who want to go to the Land That Knows No Limits? Well, what about products from the Marlboro Country Store like Snake River Fishing Gear ("An outfit made to go where the cold rivers run"), the Marlboro Folding Mountain Bike, a Mountain Lantern in Marlboro red, and the Marlboro Country Cookbook (complete with their green salsa recipe for couch cowpokes). Marlboro has so captured the iconography of cowboydom that they now have ads in mass-circulation magazines consisting *only* of recipes for such grub as Huevos Rancheros, Barkeeper's Burger, and Whiskey Beef Sandwiches.

My favorite Marlboro ad, however, is an English one in which a Harleyesque motorcycle is set out in the bleak Western plains. The only color in the bleached scene is on the bike's gas tank—Marlboro red. In art lingo, this trope is called *metonymy*.

Metonymy transfers meaning because the host image, the Marlboro cowboy, is imbedded so deep not just in American culture but in world culture that we close the circuit. Ironically, slow learners are helped by the appearance of the warning box telling you that smoking is dangerous! The Marlboro Man may indeed be Dracula to his foes, but he is still the perfect icon of adolescent independence.

Ironically, the greatest danger faced by the Marlboro Man is not from lawmen armed with scientific studies, but from some wiseguy MBA in Manhattan who will try to earn his spurs by tinkering with the campaign. This almost happened on April 22, 1993, as Michael Miles, CEO of Philip Morris, thought he could play chicken with the generics who were rustling his customers. Overnight, Miles cut the price of Marlboro by sixty cents a pack.

But the only critter he scared was the stock market, which lopped 23 percent off the price of PM stock in a single day. This day, still called "Marlboro Friday," will live in infamy as it seemed for a moment that other advertisers might follow. The whole point of branding is to make sure the consumer *pays* for the advertising by thinking that the interchangeable product is unique. He knows this when he pays a premium for it. When *Forbes* magazine (February 2, 1987) offered Marlboro smokers their chosen brand in a generic brown box at half the price, only 21 percent were interested. Just as the price of Marlboro is what economists call "inelastic," so is the advertising. Michael Miles lost his job and the company lost $13 billion in shareholder equity, but marketers learned a lesson: you don't fool with Mother Nature or a great campaign.

13

THE HATHAWAY MAN

David Ogilvy and the Branding of Branding

THE BORING, SOMEWHAT CONVENTIONAL 1950s were the most exciting time in American advertising. They almost had to be. Mass production techniques, developed in order to manufacture war materials, were now being retooled to make consumer goods. You name it, stuff from automobiles to washing machines came flying off the assembly lines and threatened to clog the arteries of the body commercial. New selling techniques had to be found. And they were.

One of the most effective ways to sell mass-produced objects (what, as mentioned earlier, are called parity items) is to create difference not in the manufacturing—after all, homogeneity is the goal of machine tooling—but in the language that surrounds them. While you cannot change what the product *is*, you can change what it *means*. And you can do this by a method as ancient as Adam in the Garden of Eden: you change the name of a thing and in so doing readjust the aura.

The ineluctable rule of human consciousness from which advertising draws its strength is that a rose by any other name would *not* smell as sweet. Glacial Springs water tastes better than Manhattan tap water, a Mustang goes faster than a Rambler, Air Jordans let you jump higher than Keds, and you call a cigarette Virginia Slims but a golf club Big Bertha.

In marketing, this naming process is called *branding*. The etymology is instructive. A brand in Anglo-Saxon is for something burned on, and came from a mark made by a hot iron on animal or human skin. We all know the scene from the Western movie

George Wrangell as the Hathaway shirt man in *The New Yorker,* 1951.

The man in the Hathaway shirt

AMERICAN MEN are beginning to realize that it is ridiculous to buy good suits and then spoil the effect by wearing an ordinary, mass-produced shirt. Hence the growing popularity of HATHAWAY shirts, which are in a class by themselves.

HATHAWAY shirts *wear* infinitely longer—a matter of years. They make you look younger and more distinguished, because of the subtle way HATHAWAY cut collars. The whole shirt is tailored more *generously*, and is therefore more *comfortable*. The tails are longer, and stay in your trousers. The buttons are mother-of-pearl. Even the stitching has an ante-bellum elegance about it.

Above all, HATHAWAY make their shirts of remarkable *fabrics*, collected from the four corners of the earth—Viyella®and Aertex® from England, woolen taffeta from Scotland, Sea Island cotton from the West Indies, hand-woven madras from India, broadcloth from Manchester, linen batiste from Paris, hand-blocked silks from England, exclusive cottons from the best weavers in America. You will get a great deal of quiet satisfaction out of wearing shirts which are in such impeccable taste.

HATHAWAY shirts are made by a small company of dedicated craftsmen in the little town of Waterville, Maine. They have been at it, man and boy, for one hundred and twenty years.

At better stores everywhere, or write C. F. HATHAWAY, Waterville, Maine, for the name of your nearest store. In New York, telephone OX 7-5566. Prices from $5.95 to $20.00.

where the young cowpokes rope and brand steers under the watchful eye of the old cowpuncher. Smoke sizzles off the red-hot iron. The calf bellows. We forget that until the nineteenth century human miscreants were also branded (*H* for hog stealer, *T* for thief) either on the skin or in the imagination (Hester Prynne's scarlet letter).

With the Industrial Revolution, the burning iron first marked shipping crates and then actual products so that retailers could be assured of expected quality and weight. Over time what started as the return address became the product name. By the 1880s, consumers were asking for their "usual brand" of cracker, tea, dungaree denim, or tobacco by name. Those brands still are burned into our consciousness as attested by Ritz, Lipton, Levi's, and Lucky Strikes.

In the 1950s, brands were rediscovered. What was slowly becoming clear was that (1) brands were being applied not just to the product but to the end-user, and (2) consumers were eager to enter affiliation with objects, regardless of how irrational it might appear. People voluntarily wore shirts with small alligators sewn on them, they drove cars with huge chromium statues on the hoods, and they would soon wear shoes with giant swoosh marks. More amazing still, they would pay extra for the magical affiliation, lots extra. A branding joke from thirty years ago: "What's in a name? A 50-percent markup."

The pivotal character in discovering this was David Ogilvy. Not only did he succeed in branding such parity items as tonic water (Schweppes), credit cards (American Express), dress shirts (Hathaway), soap (Dove), and gasoline (Shell), but he also pulled off the sublime coup of branding *himself*.

Like his creations, Ogilvy fashioned his own persona with consummate care. Part of it was very real, however. He had been kicked out of Oxford for bad grades, had worked for a while as a chef in Paris, had sold kitchen stoves door-to-door in Scotland, had farmed in Pennsylvania's Amish country, and had finally found his métier conducting surveys for George Gallup in Princeton. He entered advertising in 1949 at the age of thirty-eight with the unique ability to know not just how to collect but how to *use* market research. Ogilvy was not just a natural salesman; he actually knew what he was doing.

Whereas Thomas J. Barratt made millions by putting his brand on the literal bar of soap, Ogilvy made his by applying the brand to the entire area that surrounds the object. Once he had created this penumbra, he contended that "every advertisement should be thought of as a contribution to the brand image. It follows that your advertising should consistently project the same image: year after year" (Ogilvy 1963, 87). Once you get it down, you just sit back and collect the dividends. Or, as John Stuart, chairman of Quaker Oats, said, "If this business were to be split up, I would be glad to take the brands, trademarks, and goodwill, and you could have all the bricks and mortar—and I would fare better than you" (in Dyson et al. 1996, 9).

To see how this works, let's look at his famous ads for the Hathaway Shirt Company. They ran from 1951 to 1990, almost entirely in *The New Yorker*. Supposedly Ogilvy lost $6,000 on the account, but the shirt company cleaned up . . . at least for a while.

First, note that dress shirts are devilishly hard to brand. A white business shirt is about as fungible an object as there is—especially in the 1950s before patterns, colors, collars, elongated sleeves, and puffiness like two-tones became *de rigueur*. What can you say about a dress shirt? Made of fabric—with a body, sleeves, cuffs, a collar, buttons, tails—just like every other shirt.

So if you stuck with the shirt, all you could sell was the collar, the cuffs, or the pocket. Arrow shirts did indeed attempt to sell the collar with their famous ads in the 1930s. The Arrow Collar Man was perhaps one of the earliest and most recognizable figures popularized by dress-shirt print ads. The Gatsby-style paintings by

J. C. Leyendecker of dashing men in their high collars became symbols of the well-dressed American male.

For a while the French cuff was in fashion and was a mark of distinction. Men could now display jewelry at the wrist just like women. Elegant stores liked selling cuffs because the real money in shirts was in selling the cuff links. However, it went out in the 1930s as the Duke of Windsor announced that the *poignet mousquetaire,* or musketeer's cuff, was too formal for his taste. The cuffed shirt is now part of formal wear and power suits. For a while, J. Press attempted to make much of the buttoned flap that they put over the chest pocket, but this, too, was hardly a branding point.

Ronald Reagan as white-shirt revolutionary, 1954.

David Ogilvy had a better idea. Brand the man under the shirt, not the shirt. Now, even selling the man *in* the shirt, not the shirt, had been tried. Van Heusen had been using a second-tier Hollywood actor, Ronald Reagan, to tout the fact that its shirts "give you twice the wear of ordinary shirts," as the ad copy said, but this campaign was not really working. Women might associate glamour with movie stars, but what has a Hollywood B-movie star got to do with men's business shirts?

No, what had to happen was that the man had to appeal to women, who bought most of the men's dress shirts, while at the same time appealing to the older men who wore them. Ogilvy found just the man, a friend, Baron George Wrangell—not quite a real baron but a Russian nonetheless, who had married into a bit of money. But Ogilvy didn't quite know how to cast him. He tried, so he says, eighteen different images.

There are two versions of what happened next. If you ask the Hathaway Shirt Company (as I have), they will tell you that Edith Jetté, wife of the president of Hathaway, Ellerton Jetté, noticed a man wearing an eye patch and told her husband that the patch made any man look distinguished. Ellerton, who himself was a man of imaginative taste and a prescient collector of art, passed this on to his cub advertising agent. Ellerton Jetté was the originator of the ill-conceived slogan "Never wear a white shirt before sundown," and the introducer of the Madras shirt, and Ogilvy would have paid attention.

But Ogilvy tells a slightly different story. Here it is from his autobiography, *Confessions of an Advertising Man*:

> At first we rejected [the eye patch] in favor of a more obvious idea, but on the way to the studio I ducked into a drugstore and bought an eye patch of $1.50. Exactly why it turned out to be so successful, I shall never know. It put Hathaway on the map after 116 years of relative obscurity. What struck me as a moderately good idea for a wet Tuesday morning made me famous. I could have wished for fame to come from some more serious achievement [Ogilvy 1963, 116–17].

Ogilvy always claimed that the eye patch was really nothing more than "story appeal," a hook, and he is doubtless correct. No matter, the eye patch became to Hathaway what the wrist tattoo was to Marlboro. It was a sign of distinction, of separation, of branding. Here was a man who did not have to pretend, although admittedly he was a bit pretentious. Like Commander ("curiously refreshing") Schweppes, who sported that distinguished, well-brushed red beard, the Baron (and his successors—because the "real" Baron hightailed it back to the motherland in a few years) was just at the near edge of parody.

Ogilvy knew this. So he always cast the Baron with a touch of the Walter Mitty. In ads we saw the Baron conducting the New York Philharmonic at Carnegie Hall, copying a Goya at the Met, driving a tractor, fencing, sailing, dealing for a Renoir, all the time looking as if he were thinking about the upcoming cocktail hour.

In this ad, the most famous instance, the Baron is being fitted for bespoke tailoring. There he is with his jaunty crooked arm and look of mono-eyed hauteur staring down all who come in his path. The Hathaway man is not on his way up; this chap's already there.

Had this been the usual ad of the 1950s, the Baron would have taken up the top three-quarters of the ad space and below would have been an empty headline like "Hathaway Shirts. The finest shirts since 1837." Or (and this one, alas, is real), "True, Hathaway shirts cost a little more, but better quality always does. Nobody else makes a shirt like the Hathaway."

Not for Ogilvy. He loved to write copy, and his copy is still the best. He was a compulsive list maker. (*The Unpublished David Ogilvy*, a collection of miscellaneous speeches and memos, has an entire chapter on his lists.) While we may forget "The 13 Reasons to Buy a Rolls-Royce" (#1: "At 60 miles an hour the loudest noise comes from the electric clock"), "How Super Shell's 9 ingredients give cars top performance," or the "25 facts you should know about *KLM*," we can never forget how quickly he got us into reading the body copy.

Here's some of the body copy in this Hathaway ad. It starts:

American men are beginning to realize that it is ridiculous to buy good suits and then spoil the effect by wearing an ordinary, mass-produced shirt. Hence the growing popularity of *Hathaway* shirts, which are in a class by themselves.

Hathaway shirts *wear* infinitely longer—a matter of years. They make you look younger and more distinguished, because of the subtle way *Hathaway* cut collars. The whole shirt is tailored

> more *generously*, and is therefore more *comfortable*. The tails are
> longer, and stay in your trousers. The buttons are mother-of-pearl.
> Even the stitching has an ante-bellum elegance about it.

An "ante-bellum elegance" about stitching? What exactly does that mean? No matter, we are lined up for the famous listing. Watch as he takes the listing (what in rhetoric is called the heaping of particulars) up and over the edge into areas that only the cognoscenti could appreciate. His foot is in the door and he is jabbering. But it all seems so important.

> Above all, *Hathaway* make their shirts of remarkable *fabrics*, col-
> lected from the four corners of the earth—Viyella and Aertex
> from England, woolen taffeta from Scotland, Sea Island cotton
> from the West Indies, hand-woven madras from India, broad-
> cloth from Manchester, linen batiste from Paris, hand-blocked
> silk from England, exclusive cottons from the best weavers in
> America. You get a great deal of quiet satisfaction out of wearing
> shirts which are in such impeccable taste.

At the end, just past this peroration, Ogilvy concludes with the comment that he must have known was not true, but was true enough. Anyway, by this time the reader is too exhausted to care. In keeping with the Saville Row ethos, he claims that the shirts are made by "dedicated craftsmen . . . who have been at it man and boy for one hundred and twenty-five years." Now, I am sure they are craftsmen at Hathaway, and I am sure the shirts have been made since 1837, but in the twentieth century they have been made—as Ogilvy surely knew—not by "man and boy," but by rows of female stitchers. Women are, and have been, 95 percent of Hathaway's work force. Is this a little lie, as Picasso said, to tell the truth, or is this a little lie to reinforce a bigger one, namely that this is the dress shirt for a manly man?

Since Ogilvy, branding has become one of the mindless cants of modern marketing. Hardly a day goes by that some agency is not claiming that they can "manage the brand," "rescue the brand," "defend the brand," let alone "create the brand." A West Coast agency even claims that it understands "the soul of the brand." Much of this is self-serving mumbo-jumbo, to be sure. But just as Eskimos announce the centrality of snow by having some thirty descriptive words for crystals of frozen water, so the vocabulary explosion shows the primacy of branding.

Look at articles in professional periodicals with names like *The Journal of International Advertising Research,* and you will see more than enough jargon to make the Deconstructionists shout uncle. Since Ogilvy's ideas were taken seriously and put into pseudo-academic jargon by Burleigh Gardner and Sidney Levy in their classic *Harvard Business Review* paper of 1955, they have become the stuff of Marketing 101. There is brand personality, brand presence, brand magic, brand boundaries, brand salience, richness, esteem, and magic. Consumers are said to have unique "brandscapes" into which products must be fit.

Say what you will, we are living in the Golden Age of Brands. If the man on the street and the woman in the grocery store do not know this, they should ask their stockbroker. Thinking branded products and their brand extensions (Coke, Diet Coke, Diet Cherry Coke) are immune to economic swings, Wall Street has fallen in love with companies that can produce and maintain them. Not only are worldwide brands powering one of the greatest bull markets of modern time, not only are brands the basis of much of the merger and buyout activity of the last twenty years, but there are now companies like Sara Lee Corp., which essentially let someone else make sausages, briefcases, socks, shoe polish, and frosted cakes, while the home office nurtures the Champion, Playtex, Hanes, and Hillshire Farms brand names. Like Nike, they stitch the logo to products fabricated far away by others.

So if David Ogilvy was so smart, what happened to Hathaway? Why is it not still dominant? Ellerton Jetté sold the company to Warnaco, which sold it to private investors in Maine. Along the way it continually lost market share. Halfhearted attempts were made to resuscitate the icon (we saw Ted Turner in an eye patch, and another campaign had the Hathaway man emerging from the darkness—"After a 25 year absence he walks back into your life …"), but nothing worked. Why? Wasn't branding supposed to prevent exactly this eventuality?

What happened was that there was another wrinkle in branding. In clothing, at least, the brand has moved from the mythic man wearing the shirt to the designer of the shirt. Hathaway had unique marks—it had the largest pocket, it had three-hole mother-of-pearl buttons, and it had an embroidered red letter "H" —a subtle forerunner of today's logo-driven merchandise— hidden in the tail. But the modern customer of prestige brands wants the mark out front for all to see. Elite brands like Ralph Lauren, Gucci, Armani, Geoffrey Beene, Tommy Hilfiger, Perry Ellis, Christian Dior, and Yves Saint-Laurent have replaced the Baron, with their names and logos becoming the brand. You announce your affiliation to the surrounding world by showing that *his* initials or logo are all over your body, not your own. In the ultimate mode of branding, we enthusiastically stamp someone else's name on ourselves. Not only does Ralph Lauren give us a polo pony, he even provides an ersatz family crest!

Hathaway has now completely mothballed its icon, unable to compete with the modern souped-up designer version. In its recent ads we see a genial enough chap with a three-day-old beard smirking at us beside the headline, "Hold the Starch." What a waste of brand equity! David Ogilvy must be puffing on his pipe, looking wistfully at his vineyard in the clouds.

14

ANACIN AND THE UNIQUE SELLING PROPOSAL

How Would You Like a Hammer in the Head?

IN THE NINETEENTH CENTURY, American popular culture was carried on the back of religion. Information moved through churches. In the twentieth century, the workhorse has been commercial media. Information is carried through media partially paid for by advertising. If what you have to say in the modern world cannot be tied to a commercial message, it probably won't get through. As different as these two delivery systems may seem, however, they both promise salvation—one after death in the next world, the other right here and now in this one. *Buy* this and feel better right away replaces *believe* this and be saved later.

Sometimes the systems crisscross, and we can see how similar they both are. As one might expect, the product that brings religion and merchandising together is pain relief. After all, there is an instantaneous analogy between physical discomfort and spiritual angst. When you look at medieval paintings you see a multitude of saints experiencing the dark night of the soul. When you look at modern ads you see hundreds of adults experiencing a wincing head pain. While *malaise* used to mean fear of perdition, it now means a high fever.

Painkilling medicine similar to aspirin has actually been used at least since the fifth century B.C., when Hippocrates used a bitter powder made from willow bark to treat aches. But it wasn't until 1897 that a German chemist synthesized the powder, acetylsalicylic acid, and the Bayer company bottled it, named it aspirin, and sent it off to market.

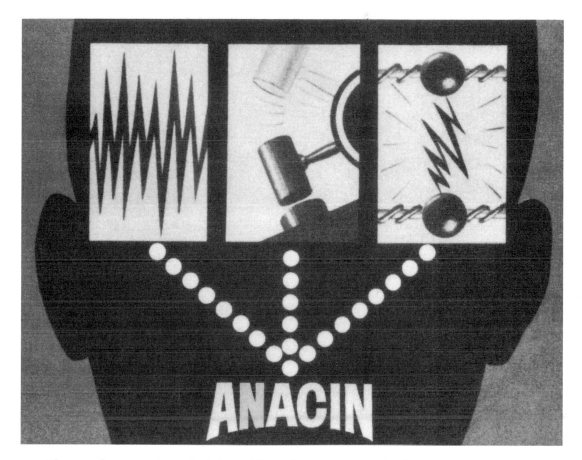

The product was branded, literally, with BAYER in the shape of—dare I say it?—the cross. In fact, when the company shifted production in 1914 from a powdered form to a tablet form, the company proudly called the logo the "Bayer Cross" (B-A-Y-E-R spelled vertically and horizontally, intersecting at the letter Y). Some religious groups complained about the sacrilege.

Although Bayer may have known the religious overtones of pain relief, they really didn't know how to sell it. So they promoted the product to doctors who would pass this information on to patients. Once the patent protection was lost, Anacin, the upstart, knew better. It advertised to the end-users, the afflicted, who would then demand that the pharmacist carry the specific product.

In understanding the importance of marketing, Anacin joins the legion of companies who arrive late at the dance, but end up with the belle of the ball. Just showing up first doesn't guarantee success. Remember Du Pont's Corfam, Gablinger's beer, the Convair 880, Vote toothpaste, Sperry-Rand's Univac, and Sony's Betamax? You have to get on the consumer's dance card. And to do that you have to position yourself.

Anacin positioned itself as powerful pain medicine. The dominant Anacin campaign began in the 1940s on radio. Anacin's radio spots proclaimed that the substance was "like a doctor's prescription—not just one but a combination of several medically active ingredients." When the ads jumped into visual media with the television ads of the mid-1950s, they showed how a real nasty headache really works. Upstairs in your head is a hammer that bangs into an anvil. This anvil chorus is so diabolical that it can turn a saint into a sinner. Relief can indeed be blessed. We know this salvation is possible because again and again we saw the same tableau on television of a mom made demonic by a headache and then made angelic by Anacin.

Who was more saintly in those years than Mom? Watching this female Dr. Jekyll let her ferocious self out of Hyding while experiencing the dreaded "tension" headache was a frightful experience. How would you like it if your mom were in such terrible shape that she would close her eyes in pain, massage her temples, and then explode, "Can't you play someplace else?" And all you were doing at the time was playing quietly with your stuffed animals.

Good thing Mom's superego came to the rescue, saying, in an angelic version of her own voice, "Control yourself. Sure, you have a headache, but don't take it out on him." And following this voice comes another, a man's voice from on high. "You need Anacin for fast relief. The big difference in Anacin makes a big difference in the way you feel."

This last voice, the disembodied voice held over from radio days, now delivers what the ad was all about: the famous Unique

Selling Proposal. This Voice of Authority tells how to stop the pounding hammer, uncoil the spring, and unplug the lightning bolt—all pictured so graphically in the skull-rattling illustration.

God-as-Doctor-as-Announcer tells us that "Anacin is like a doctor's prescription—that is, a combination of ingredients; the pain reliever most recommended by doctors plus an extra ingredient missing from leading aspirins, still missing with buffering, combined in Anacin to relieve pain, to relax tension, and sooth irritability." We who are in our fifties know this refrain as well as we know what is inside a Big Mac.

The little morality play of Anacin advertising (sin, guilt, divine intercession, redemption) was probably the most hated ad of all time. It makes "Stop squeezing the Charmin," "How 'bout a Hawaiian Punch," and "Ring around the collar" look like playground exercises.

You couldn't get away from this ad. During the Cuban missile crisis, while we were biting our fingernails in nuclear-bomb anxiety, Walter Cronkite interrupted the broadcast with "And now a word for Anacin." Talk about a segue to the surreal.

Say what you want, this migraine of a campaign also increased sales from $18 million to $54 million in just eighteen months. Rosser Reeves of the Ted Bates Agency bragged to *The New Yorker* that just the spot with the skull bangers "made more money for the producers of Anacin in seven years than *Gone With the Wind* did for David O. Selznick and MGM in a quarter of a century" (Whiteside 1969, 47). It cost all of $8,200 to produce.

Why was it so successful? First, of course, it makes a dead-on-target claim. Anacin is *like* a doctor's prescription. The simile is made metaphoric, however, by the visual analog. For as we hear the announcer, we see three dishes of powdered analgesic being sucked back into the package. This stuff does have added ingredients! We can see them being added. Who cares if the added ingredient is caffeine (wisely not mentioned as the secret ingredient); the point is that it has *more than* the other pain relievers *plus* the pain reliever most recommended by doctors, namely, aspirin!

In his best-selling *Reality in Advertising* (1961), Reeves explained what separated his technique from the celebrated claim-staking of his predecessor Claude Hopkins. Hopkins said it didn't matter what you said as long as you said it first. Who cares if all brewers clean their bottles with steam as long as the consumer thinks that only your product does it? The competition always will be perceived as a Johnny-come-lately. Reeves said that what you say must be inherent in the product and relate to customers' needs by promising a clear benefit. In fact, when you think about it, Hopkins and Reeves were both defining what "positioning" is all about.

But to think that the Unique Selling Proposal is why the Anacin ad worked is to miss what's really going on. Reeves, raised in a strict Methodist family, knew the power of repetition, the power of invocation, and the power of prayer. As John Lyden, his colleague at Bates, commented without really knowing the significance, "[Reeves] was a Methodist turned inside out" (in Fox 1984, 189).

Once you have the mantra, never let it go. Just keep spinning the prayer wheel. Reeves's mentor, Claude Hopkins, had a more pastoral analogy. He said about repetition, "You cannot chop a tree in two by hitting it every time in a different place." Reeves ran this ad, and variations of it, for years and years and years. "Originality," as Reeves said, "is the most dangerous word in advertising."

There was a perhaps apocryphal tale about a time when Reeves was out sailing with a client. The client made bold to ask why he should continue paying the same fee when the ad was never really changed. "What do you need all those people on my account when you never *do* anything?" Reeves, who could be surly, gruffed, "To keep your people from changing what I've done." More famously, Reeves wagered he could sell more by using a mediocre ad repeated ad nauseam than by using a good ad that had to be changed every six months.

Reeves knew more than the power of incantation. He instinctively knew the power of threes. Just as Christianity has the Father, the Son, and the Holy Ghost, the Anacin ads are filled with triplets. Here are just a few: the three icons raising hell in the skull; the three dishes with the added ingredients; the three bold words on the package, "Fast Pain Relief," and below them in boldface: "Headache, Neuralgia, Neuritis" (whatever the hell the last two are—they were never explained); the three promises "Stops headache! Relieves tension! Calms jittery nerves!"; the three product claims:

relieve pain

relax tension

sooth irritability

and, of course, the announcer's insistent tag line, "For fast, Fast, FAST relief...."

The Age of Anacin is long gone. Instead of getting a headache from the ad, you get a headache from the explosion of products. Once the battle was between Bayer (now made by Sterling Winthrop), which was the textbook example of how a product can go from laboratory to branded product, and Anacin (from American Home Products), which was the example of how advertising can show how a branded product works. Then came Bufferin (Bristol-Myers), which showed how you can take an aspect of the product and claim you do it better, in this case faster. In one promotion we were told that "Bufferin combines aspirin with two antacid ingredients which open the stomach valve, getting the pain reliever into the bloodstream twice as fast as aspirin. So Bufferin acts twice as fast as aspirin to relieve pain." For years we watched the little B's scoot around the stomach faster than the slow-motion A's. If you watch carefully, you will see that the B's are moving exactly twice as fast.

The Age of Anacin really ended in 1976 with the classic parity claim from Tylenol (Johnson & Johnson): "You can't buy a more potent pain reliever without a prescription." What they didn't say is that for average headaches, the claim is equally true when it comes to Tylenol's competitors. The phrase seems to say "We're the best," but it actually means "We're the same." In fact, in an irony worthy of Reeves, whenever you see something advertised as "Unsurpassed!" or "Unbeaten!" it most likely means that this product is on an equal footing with its competition.

The pleasure's gone out of pain relief. When you have to parse a recent statement like "Anacin relieves headache pain better than regular-strength Bayer or Bufferin," you know that the copy is being written by CPAs. No parity in this claim; it says flatly that Anacin relieves pain better. What you aren't told, however, is that a souped-up Anacin tablet has 23 percent more aspirin in it than the regular-strength tablet of its competitors. Anacin is slightly more effective because it has slightly more medicine. No fair!

Or what of "More hospitals trust Tylenol"? Well, hospitals do use Tylenol, and when you think about it, they would be unlikely to give out something they didn't trust. But why Tylenol? Could it be because Johnson & Johnson sells the drug to hospitals at such a steep discount that they would be fools to turn it down? In fact, this is one reason they're able to make the claim, "Hospitals use Tylenol eighteen times more than all ibuprofen brands combined."

The pain-relief market is now so crowded that pain itself has been recalibrated, more the result of the advertising for analgesics than by differing physical ailments. Since relief has become such an interchangeable item, such a sinkhole for festering claims, you now sell the pain, not the cure. How else to account for Excedrin headache #23?

There's just too much to choose from: there's aspirin, acet-aminophen (the generic name for Tylenol), and non-aspirin NSAIDs, or non-steroidal anti-inflammatory drugs, such as ibu-profen (the generic name for Advil, Motrin, and others), ketopro-fen (the generic name for Actron, Orudis KT, and others), and naproxen sodium (the generic name for Aleve). This stuff comes in regular-strength, extra-strength, maximum-strength; daytime formulations, nighttime formulations, and children's formulations. You can take it in pills, gel caps, liquid formulations, suppositories, injections, powders, and even transdermal patches.

Worse yet, each of these products now has its own Unique Selling Proposition: the "no-upset-stomach" painkiller, the "you can't buy a more potent pain reliever without a doctor's prescrip-tion," the "one of ours is worth two of theirs," the kind that "two out of three doctors recommend," the ones that "hospitals prefer" or that "Dr. Mom" prescribes, and, of course, all those Excedrin headaches. Enough already!

What brought the curtain down on Reeves and USP was not the profusion of parity products and their differing claims. Nor was it the constant badgering of the Food and Drug Administra-tion. Nor was it the suave image-advertising of Reeves's brother-in-law David Ogilvy, or the lightly ironic approach of Bernbach, or even the tidal wave of California-cool "advertainment." What did in repetitious Reeves was the technical wizardry of the remote-control clicker. Power moved from the voice of the godlike announcer inside the TV set to the wand in the palm of the god-like viewer. The next sound you hear after the announcer starts the litany of USP is ... *click!* The hand-held remote was the cross to the too-often-returning vampire. RIP.

15

LBJ VS. BARRY GOLDWATER

Thirty-Second Politics

THERE ARE THREE KINDS of political ads: positive, comparative, and negative. The positive tells what a great guy you are, the comparative proves it, and the negative says what a rapscallion your opponent is, thereby letting the voter draw the inevitable inferences about you. Or so you hope.

Listening to pundits discuss negative advertising, you might think that these nasty sound-and-sight bites are a new scourge carried by electronic culture. Not so. Throwing mud is the oldest of American political traditions, right behind tar-and-feathering. All that has really changed is the delivery system.

Recall that opponents of Thomas Jefferson claimed that if he was elected, "the Bible will be burned ... and we may see our wives and daughters the victims of legal prostitution"; that Andrew Jackson was attacked for his wife's alleged bigamy, adultery, and promiscuity (she failed to properly divorce her first husband); that Lincoln was called a "Liar, Thief and Buffoon" in *Harper's Weekly*; that opponents of Grant distributed a one-inch metal pig, worn as a charm around the neck (when one held it to the light, one could look through a hole below the pig's tail and see a picture of Grant inside); that Cleveland was accused of fathering an illegitimate child, an act celebrated in torchlight parades where Republicans chanted "Ma, Ma, where's my Pa?", and, well, you get the point.

It has often been said that "he who slings dirt loses the most ground," but in the modern world the populace may be at more risk from the positive campaign than from the negative. The self-

"Daisy"

1   Little girl: 1, 2, 3, 4, 5, 7, 6, 6 . . .

2   Little girl: 8, 9, 9 . . .

3   (VO) 10, 9, 8, 7, 6, 5, 4, 3, 2, 1, 0

4   (VO) These are the stakes: to make a world in which all of God's children can live or go into the dark.

5   (VO) We must either love each other or we must die.

6   (VO) The stakes are too high for you to stay home.

VOTE FOR PRESIDENT JOHNSON ON NOVEMBER 3.

Vote for President Johnson . . . or else:
DDB's "Daisy," 1964.

inflating, pandering ad passes us by with no warning flags flying, no truth buzzers blaring. No newspaper ever devoted a critical column to Reagan's rhapsodic "Morning Again in America" campaign. It seemed so comforting, so pleasant to hear the dulcet voice of adman Hal Riney telling us how great things were. Yet in many ways it was deceitful to see America as a continuation of Phil Dusenberry's Pepsi campaign and as powerful as any negative ad could be.

A few years later, however, we howled at Bush's negative ads showing Michael Dukakis, looking just like Rocky the Flying Squirrel, driving a tank in circles. And we were upset by his revolving turnstile ad implying that Dukakis had set Willie Horton free to ravage innocent citizens.

It is an irony worthy of our times that we have learned to override the attack ad. We have *not* learned to suspect the self-congratulatory one—at least not yet.

The negative ad that started the inoculation process would have to be Lyndon Baines Johnson's 1964 ad attacking Barry Goldwater. This most compressed and noxious political ad ever made derives some of its power from the fact that it never mentions Senator Goldwater by name. In fact, in a television documentary called "The Classics of Political Television Advertising," Senator Eugene McCarthy calls it "the most effective media campaign in American history," in part because the viewer does all the nasty work. Semiologists have to take Prozac to view it. It is a work of awful beauty.

We open on a young Caucasian girl in a daisy field, pulling petals from a daisy stem. She looks just like Little Maria in James Whale's 1931 *Frankenstein*. You may remember that Little Maria is also out picking flowers when she is met by the monster. The lumbering Boris Karloff, with head sutures and neck bolt, plays with Maria for a while. Maria tosses her flower into the lake. "I can make a boat," she says. The monster does the same with his flower, and they both marvel at the floating flowers. Soon the flowers drift away and the monster, never losing a beat, picks up Little Maria and wings her out into the lake, where she does not float. This last scene was thankfully cut from the studio version, but we know what has happened because we all remember seeing her father marching through the streets carrying the wet little bundle that was once his Little Maria. In the background, all the townspeople are shrieking bloody revenge against the monster.

Well, in the Democratic version from the 1964 campaign, our Little Maria is approached from below—just the opposite of the Frankenstein POV and just as off-putting. As we move toward her, she is slowly pulling off daisy petals from the stem. The camera moves up from ground level as we hear her counting off the snapped petals. "One … two … three," and now we are moving up her front, "five … seven … six … six," and, while she stumbles, we are focused on her face, "eight … nine." At the stroke of "ten," we move to her eye, which is now a black orb. As we are going *into* her eye, a new voice takes over. This is the voice of Mission Control, reversing the process with metronomic efficiency as the camera presses ahead into the darkness: "10-9-8-7-6…" No missed numbers this trip. This guy is all business. As we go deeper into her black eye, we hear the number "1" in dispassionate tones and see first the explosion, then the mushroom cloud, and then the fierce firestorm covering all the screen.

For those of us who grew up in the 1960s, this sequence is as well known as the presidential motorcade that day in Dallas or the pictures of the earth shot from the moon. The Atomic Bomb monster is loose and we are all shrieking bloody murder.

Now we hear the nasal voice of LBJ quoting W. H. Auden: "These are the stakes: to make a world in which all of God's children can live or to go into the dark. We must either love each other or we must die." Cut to the final black panel with a new voice, the voice of the godlike announcer who is usually selling us underarm deodorant: "The stakes are too high for you to stay home. Vote." And then, reading from the white letters: "Vote for President Johnson on November third."

This ad was shown only once, on September 7, 1964, during a break in *David and Bathsheba*, NBC's "Monday Night at the Movies." That is, "Daisy" was shown only once as a paid advertisement, but these thirty seconds were repeated ad nauseam on news programs, even making it to the cover of *Time* magazine.

And in so doing, "Daisy" set the path of attack ads: ideally your ad gets seen by the voter not by paying your way, but by raising such a ruckus that the media, especially television news, does the donkey work for you. This is one of the reasons why political consultants go for "news adjacencies," the commercial slots before and after a newcast. Not only are people who watch the news likely to vote, they are likely to associate the commercial with the news. Get lucky and your commercial becomes the news.

In true new-style fashion, the "Daisy" campaign started with Aaron Ehrlich, a producer with DDB, meeting with radio adman Tony Schwartz. "Would you work for this product?" Ehrlich asked Schwartz, holding up a picture of LBJ (in Diamond and Bates 1984, 127). Schwartz, who had done one of the best Coke ads ever (which featured dew dripping from two frosty bottles behind a wordless soundtrack of undifferentiated human play noises) knew what the job was.

The early 1960s were rife with the frantic imagery of paranoia. Not only did the Russians have the bomb, they were going to use it. Goldwater's great mistake was that he couldn't stop talking about this. He had talked about dropping low-yield nuclear bombs on the supply lines in North Vietnam "so we can see who was under the trees"; he had joked about dropping a "nuke" into the men's room at the Kremlin, and, worse yet, he had called the nuclear bomb "merely another weapon." He was forever posing in the cockpits of fighter planes, looking like something out of *Dr.*

Strangelove. Goldwater even ran an ad in which a group of schoolchildren are reciting the Pledge of Allegiance until their voices are drowned out by a thundering Nikita Khrushchev, who proclaims in Russian: "We will bury you! Your children will be Communists!"

So, in a way, Goldwater asked for "Daisy." Just as, in a way, he almost invited the recasting of his slogan of "In your heart, you know he's right" into "In your guts, you know he's nuts."

Although Mr. Schwartz now regrets his packaging and has gone apostate in his *The Responsive Chord*, he really is not to blame. Actually, Nelson Rockefeller laid the pipe between about-to-go-ballistic Goldwater and Armageddon by continually harping on this during the Republican primary. All Schwartz did was connect the dots.

Or, better yet, he let the viewer connect the Hiroshima dots. As he himself has said, this ad "was the first national Rorschach test. It was not what the ad said, but what people thought it said that made it so effective. This was a positive ad about the dangers of nuclear war [but] it was perceived as an anti-Goldwater ad because of statements he had made about nuclear weapons" (in Burdan and Meyer 1989, 37).

The other individual responsible for this ad is the ever-genial, ever-earnest (and ever-embarrassed for his collusion) Bill Moyers. Although Mr. Moyers went on to host PBS shows like *A Walk Through the 20th Century*, in which he gasps at how advertising is exploiting our innocent desires, such was not always his response. In fact, "Daisy" was *his* baby.

Moyers was LBJ's press secretary, and DDB had to get this ad through his office. No problem because it was Moyers himself who suggested that the agency raise the nuclear issue against Goldwater. Finally, a half-century after the campaign, Moyers confessed. Here he is responding to a question from Jane Hall of the *Los Angeles Times*:

Q. When you were an aide to Lyndon Johnson, did you approve the infamous "Daisy" commercial?

A. Yes I did, and I regret that we were in on the first wave of the future. The ad was intended to remind voters of Johnson's prudence; it wasn't meant to make you think Barry Goldwater was a war monger—but that's how a lot of people interpreted it. If my memory serves me correctly, we never touched on Vietnam in any of the political spots. It haunts me all this time that Johnson was portrayed as the peacemaker in that campaign, but he committed the country to a long, bloody war in Vietnam [Hall 1989, 4].

Use your own judgment about the intention to spin Goldwater as a "war monger." Goldwater himself was always furious that Moyers disavowed responsibility, saying that Moyers "has lectured us on truth, the public trust, a fairer and finer America [but] every time I see him, I get sick to my stomach and want to throw up" (Ferguson 1991, 22). Then Goldwater went on to pay DDB and Schwartz the ultimate compliment, saying that this campaign was "enough to make me vote Democratic, if I had not known their nominee so well."

Rosser Reeves, the granddaddy of political advertising, concurred. He said he pictured a mushroom cloud rising up from behind Barry Goldwater's head whenever he recalled "Daisy." Such a great ad lives forever, not just in Political Advertising 101, but in countless resurrections. Like the Frankenstein monster, it won't die.

It recently came shuffling forth in a Bob Dole version. We see the same clip of the little girl picking daisies, but a new voice speaks: "Thirty years ago the biggest threat to her was nuclear war. Today the threat is drugs. Teenage drug use has doubled in the last four years. What's been done?" Now we segue not to the mushroom cloud but to such images as a needle in an arm and a kid with a crack pipe—the contemporary equivalent of a nuclear holocaust.

Who but agency fools and network toadies have ever come to the defense of this kind of political advertising? Yet I think two matters need to be addressed. First, voters are not really taken in by such ads; in fact, we now expect them. We expect Act 3 of any campaign to begin, "Enter stage left: Guerrilla Media."

And, second, like it or not, we live in a world in which politics, not just elections, is conducted *on* television *in* your living room. While it is nice to reminisce about public discussion of important matters, entire subjects like health insurance, taxation, or even small wars are compressed into thirty seconds. Images are moved into the place of argument. Don't say we're going back to the Persian Gulf: cue the "smart bomb" footage.

In 1968, presidential candidate Richard Nixon was waiting to appear on *The Mike Douglas Show*. He complained to Roger Ailes, then a producer on the talk show, that "it's too bad a guy has to rely on a gimmick like television to get elected." Ailes, now head of Fox News, knew better: "Television is not a gimmick, and nobody will ever be elected to major office again without knowing how to use it" (Hall 1996, E01).

"Daisy" was no gimmick. It did not trivialize an issue; it just blew it up. And Goldwater along with it.

16

SHE'S VERY CHARLIE

The Politics of Scent

ON WALL STREET it is said that you are never really any good at corporate research until you can make money by investing in airline stocks. On Madison Avenue the same can be said about advertising perfumes. Selling smells—or, better yet, selling the *meaning* of a smell—is the pure form of the art, the place where theory goes out the window and genius takes over. Perfume is sizzle, very little steak.

The competition to get your sizzle smelled and out of the store is fierce. That's why all those young ladies are enthusiastically spritzing as you enter your local department store. It has taken lawsuits to get them to quit hosing down their clientele without first asking. And that's why all those ladies' magazines are so thick. Next time you are near a coffee table, heft a copy of *Vogue* or *Cosmopolitan*. Open at the first spread, then turn the page. Turn again, and again, and once more—chances are that you will have just been beaten about the nostril by a relentless stream of commercial messages from numerous perfumeries.

Every year hundreds of new perfumes are introduced, and they almost all have to make their way to our nostrils through these pages and inside department stores. You may be able to support a perfume on television, but you need print and aggressive department store spritzers (for lack of a better word) to introduce it. There may be word of mouth for most products, but there is no word of nose for perfumes.

Nasal clutter, called "fragrance abuse" in the trade, has only been made worse by the advent of the "scent strip." After much

The fanny pat from Charlie, the feminist, 1970s to 1980s.

SHE'S VERY CHARLIE.

Charlie

REVLON

to-do and some legal arm-twisting from asthmatics, *The New Yorker* has none of them. As perfumers know, the nose knows only about three smells before it starts gasping for fresh air. That's why professional smellers (called "noses") often carry bags of coffee beans so they can blot out extraneous smells and start over.

So if you follow the invocations of these ads to "pull the tab to release fragrance and fantasies," "indulge in the compelling scent of Obsession," or "have a Forbidden fling," which invite us to open the fold covering the perfume sample, you soon learn what Marcel Proust knew. Once loosed, the smell lingers in memory only if it can find quick associations. Gen-Xers have a nifty phrase, "boning the magazine," which refers to wrestling out these odious inserts—especially the scent strips—so that the magazine can be rendered readable.

In a sense, the strip is the tribute that smell pays to memory, for the images of most perfumes are as redundant and short-lived as the smells. That's why the most expensive scent strip for the advertiser is the first one you encounter in the magazine.

The enormous value of the global market in little drops of odoriferous water and the fascination perfume holds for those who market it, plus, of course, our participation as consumers in this almost "virtual" industry, is explained by the unacknowledged importance of smell. While we often think of smell as the least of the senses, the one we could most easily do without, the sense controls the two most basic animal instincts: self-preservation and reproduction. Yuck, we say when we are too close to carrion. Yummy, we say when we are not close enough to pleasure.

Smell is base and primitive. It doesn't fool around with the other senses. In fact, en route to memory, it goes directly to a central point in the brain—the olfactory bulb. Other senses are mediated, not smell.

Smells literally attract us and repel us. I mean that physically. This may be why we have such trouble describing smells (in the trade, description is done in terms of "notes," as in "top notes" and "bottom notes," almost like music), but we have little trouble telling how smells make us feel. Little wonder that car dealers spray the smell of new leather through their cars, that real-estate agents tell you to bake something in the kitchen before showing your house, and that the hot new field in feeling good about yourself is called aromatherapy. Ditto the booming business in removing what Madison Avenue has convinced us are bad smells: BO, halitosis, and vaginal odor.

Smells are initially detected by a tiny vomeronasal receptor nestled deep in our noses, snuggled up against the septum an inch inside the nostril. As we have evolved, this detector has been getting smaller. Our eyes now do the work of our nostrils. We have only a dim understanding of how important whiffing and sniffing has been for us in the past. When looking at deer snorting the air or donkeys urinating on their own legs, we think, *How curious, how animalistic.* Then we splash on a little Brut or Obsession and head for the dance floor.

Monkeys lose their interest in mating when their noses are plugged. We do, too, although we don't usually admit it. All you have to do, however, is glance at advertising for cold remedies to see how pathetically un-potent we are when stuffed up.

Take the central act of courtship, the kiss. There is no doubt that the kiss, for all the displaced resonance of what bodies do during coitus, is also a way to get our little smell detector up next to our partner and give them a once-over. Does our future partner smell bad? Could s/he be sick, diseased, rotten? Eskimos know what they are doing. Many anthropologists believe that rubbing noses is what the kiss once was, and makes clear what the kiss is all about. Scientists have theorized that in the past we also smelled hands as a way to detect attraction/revulsion, which is where the practice of handshakes and kissing the hand may originate.

Since human females don't go into estrus, we don't know exactly what smells attract the sexes. For a long time we thought that attraction was triggered by floral scents. How romantic! Although we have forgotten why young swains come courting with flowers in hand, this is part of the reason. Then we thought the attraction might be instigated by glandular secretions, similar to those given off by animals in heat, so we became obsessed with slaughtering deer for their musk glands. How atavistic! There is now an after-shave called Score, which advertises that it is built of pheromones. You can't buy Score in stores—too dangerous—so you must call an 800 number instead.

Now we think that scent triggers must come from the apocrine glands, which contribute to the scent of human sweat, urine, breath, saliva, breast milk, skin oils, and sexual secretions. These glands occur in dense concentrations on hands, cheeks, scalp, breast areolas, and wherever we possess body hair, and are only turned "on" after puberty when we begin searching for mates.

But, amazingly, they can also be turned "off" for certain pairings. I say *certain* pairings because it seems that the smell of our relatives is a turn-off. How do we know this? Because hundreds of men and women have been asked to smell special cotton underwear of members of the opposite sex, and general feelings of well-being increase as smells come from more and more distant relatives. Ovulating women have especially acute sensitivity to certain familial smells. Could smell be connected to incest aversion? To recast the old phrase, familiarity not only breeds contempt, it may not want to breed at all.

I mention all this complexity because, while we know that we are excited by smells, we do not know exactly which smells are really picked up by the ever-alert nostril of love. The word *perfume* should clue us in to what is moving up to the brain every time we inhale. Perfume means "blown through smoke" (from the Latin *per fumare*) and has its roots in the burning of gummy spices called incense. And it should not be missed that this word *incense* means both "aromatic substance" as a noun and "arouse" as a verb.

All this explosive paradox adheres to the history of perfume advertising. While the Egyptians were the first pioneers in aromatherapy, and there are Biblical references to the use of anointed and perfumed oils, in the modern world it is the French who have taken over the manufacture. It is the Americans, however, who know how to sell the paradox.

Modern perfume advertising really started just before World War II as French designers came to realize that there was money to be made telling stories to women about smell. The stories were about love and conquest, and they were tied to the effect of a smell on a man. Looking at the ads from the 1930s and 1940s, you can see that this body incense is described as enchanting, inviting, alluring, and captivating. Products generally had exotic names: Shalimar, Joy, Trésor, and L'Air du Temps. This was the time when Christian Dior rewarded his exclusive clientele with a new fragrance at the end of a show, and Coco Chanel gave away bottles of No. 5 (supposedly named for a batch of super-strong aldehyde) as a gesture of thanks. Soon they were selling it. And perfume was becoming an extension of couture.

After the war, multinational companies got into the business: Unilever, which produces washing powders, kitchen cleaners, and Calvin Klein's CK One, Elizabeth Arden's Red Door, and

Elizabeth Taylor's White Diamonds; Procter & Gamble, which manufactures baby food and Max Factor's Le Jardin; and French conglomerates like Elf, which produces engine oil and the Yves Saint Laurent fragrances. They realized that if you spent lots more on the packaging and advertising, you could spend lots less on the "juice," as they started to call it. Better yet, the market seemed to be able to absorb a steady flow not of new smells, but of new pitches. You could tie the juice to a movie star, a clothing designer, or an abstract concept like forbidden love, and instead of glutting the market, you would expand it. Perfume was becoming less of a smell and more of a commodity.

The name of the game was rapidly becoming the game of naming. First you got the name, then the image, and finally, almost as an afterthought, the fragrance. Names were scooped up and trademarked as the conglomerates realized it was not enough to have a reservoir of "aspirationals" like True Love, Wings, and Escape; you had to drain the supply from your competition. When Guerlain, Inc., launched Samsara, the company considered over 50,000 names before choosing a somewhat obscure Sanskrit word meaning "everlasting" or "journeying." Even so the name had already been registered. Poets were hired to coin names like Amarige, by Parfums Givenchy, meant to conjure mirages, magic, marvelous encounters, and … marriage.

But the best way to a perfect name was to have such a finely tuned antenna to the shifting sea changes of popular culture that you could find a distant tsunami and ride it all the way to shore. No one currently does this better than Calvin Klein. Who else knew to bring out Obsession in the 1980s, then Escape in the early 1990s, and the unisex CK One for today. This split-second marketing for scents that "last through the ages" started not with Calvin but with Charlie, Revlon's launch of a new jasmine-loaded scent in the late 1960s.

In a world where French names were *de rigueur,* the use of a male diminutive was startling. Many people thought "Charlie" was the last gasp of Charles Revson, the ailing CEO, who was, in his last days, naming products after himself. Many insiders were concerned about the name. But not the customers. They liked it.

More startling to the customers was that the "Charlie" woman in the ads was younger than the usual perfume user. She was invariably pictured in the daytime, doing something *active,* and often doing it alone, like strutting around in front of the Eiffel Tower, hitching a ride on a luggage dolly in a hotel lobby, striding down a city street in a mannish tweed suit and boots with three-inch heels, or apparently nude in the water with nothing showing but an upswept hairdo and a pearl necklace. In fact, if men are in the picture, they are usually looking at her with awe, often with their faces blurred.

If she is with a recognizable man, as we see in this most famous example, the microecology of social relationships is profoundly rearranged. She's in charge. No doubt about it. For appreciators of irony, it might be noted that while the model for those ever-so-successful Charlie ads occasionally wore trousers, Mr. Revson wouldn't allow his women employees to wear trousers to work.

But in the magical world of advertising, Charlie is not just in charge, she is clearly enjoying dominance. She is taller than her partner, more confident. Presumably they are both going back to their respective offices (note that they carry the same sized work tools, the ubiquitous attaché case, and wear the same black-and-white business attire), but they are not of equal status. As they are saying their ta-ta's, she looks down, he looks askance. Not only does he have part of his anatomy removed from the picture so that the Charlie bottle can be foregrounded, and not only does she have the jaunty scarf and the cascading hair of a free spirit, but she is delivering that most masculine of signifiers, the booty pat.

The booty pat in this image is what the kiss is in the usual perfume ad. But the booty pat is most usually seen being delivered man to man, leader to follower, in a very controlled environment, usually an athletic event. In football especially, the pat signifies comradeship, dedication to business, and is applied dominant to submissive. After throwing his arm around the shoulder of a player, the coach delivers it to a hulking cub who is returning to the field of battle. After breaking the huddle, the quarterback delivers it to his massive linemen. When Charlie bestows it on her gentleman friend here in Downtown U.S.A., she is harvesting a rich crop of meaning. The tide has turned, and now men are getting their butts slapped by, of all people, women. Charlie has subverted sexism, turned it on its head, used it against itself, and she knows it.

The New York Times knew it as well and the editors initially refused to run the ad, saying it was in "poor taste." But eleven women's magazines knew better and did indeed recognize that often "poor taste" is just another word for "something really important going on." What was going on was, of course, the women's movement, and Charlie was out in front. She was giving the Old Spice man his sailing orders, and he was enjoying it.

Charlie was also becoming something else. She was becoming the designer name for a new audience, the eponymic celebrity who links maker's persona to user's. You can see these strands of marketing coming together in the 1970s.

On one hand, there is the French or Italian designer "name" (never British or German!) like "Coco" Chanel (who was the first couturier to use her own name on a perfume) followed by Dior, Oleg Cassini, Christian Lacroix, et al., all the way up to Giorgio Armani and the Americans Ralph Lauren, Tommy Hilfiger, and Calvin Klein. The name becomes the signature fragrance. Their perfumes are metaphors for their style.

On the other hand, there is the celebrity scent. Chanel found this out quite by accident. Back in the 1950s there was a famous photograph of Marilyn Monroe tipping a bottle of Chanel No. 5 into her cleavage. She was famously quoted as saying that this was the only thing she ever wore in bed. Chanel sales soared. It was only a matter of time before Sophia Loren lent her name to a fragrance, and it was adios Paris designer and bonjour Hollywood star. For some 3 to 5 percent of the action, celebrities have been tripping over themselves to market their own fragrances—Joan Collins, Elizabeth Taylor, Jaclyn Smith, Candice Bergen, Julio Iglesias, Princess Stephanie of Monaco, Gabriela Sabatini, Priscilla Presley, and Michael Jordan.

Charlie got it both ways. She's a designer name, the image of Revlon style. And she's a celebrity—the take-charge woman entering the workplace. Mal MacDougall, who worked on the campaign for the agency Hill, Holliday, Connors, Cosmopulos, has said that nothing so sophisticated was going on in his mind when he and his creative partner, Catherine Campbell, were leafing through stacks of photos, seeking models with the right look for Charlie. They just got into the habit of saying, "She's a Charlie," when they thought they spotted the type. She's sexy, to be sure, but she's not concerned about it.

As opposed to the usual perfume ad of the 1960s and 1970s, "sex is not everything to a girl who wears Charlie," Mr. MacDougall explained. "But she's as good at it as anybody else" (Dougherty 1986, 7). What Charlie is really good at, however, is that she balances sex and work. And this is what made millions for Revlon. For Charlie was not a wear-once-a-week-and-buy-a-bottle-every-other-Christmas perfume, but one to wear every day. You wore it to work. In fact, Charlie started a genre of smell called "elevator emptiers," perfume for women that was what after-shave was for men. What this term also means is that the executive elevator was carrying a new kind of "suit." Thanks to Charlie.

Little wonder that Revlon panicked as they saw their Charlies move through the demographic wave of the baby boom and then start wearing T-shirts with sentiments like "Oh my God, I forgot to have children!" Under the genius of Michel Bergerac, Revlon's suave, French-born chairman in the 1970s, Revlon extended the family line to include Charlie's younger sisters like Charlie Red, Charlie White, and Charlie Gold. There is even Charlie Sunshine for teenyboppers.

And what of Charlie Original? Although for a while this was the best-selling perfume in the world, the core users are now in their fifties and most have dumped the brand. Revlon has retired "She's Very Charlie." It no longer shocks a generation that has been very Charlie since birth, and is still moving into the board-room. But this campaign, along with such stalwarts as Maiden-form's memorable Dream campaign ("I dreamed I was a ... in my Maidenform bra"), Clairol's "Does She ... or Doesn't She?" and Virginia Slims' "You've Come a Long Way, Baby," shows that when you are selling something that is just like all its competitors, you forget the product and talk politics.

Although many in the women's movement have blamed advertising for exploiting women, causing anorexia, excoriating fat, touting cosmetics and dangerous surgery, it should also be recognized that Madison Avenue is always more amoral than immoral. To a considerable degree—a degree not yet acknowl-edged in popular culture—advertising provided the imagery of the new woman, striving not strident, proud of her accomplishments and not afraid to say so, and, most of all, not anything like the dour "make room for me, or else" libber of the argumentative media. In fact, front and center in the biggest single shift in American social values since the end of World War II—namely the acceptance of women in the workplace—was this twenty-something with a booty pat. Hardly the image of revolution, but she was revolution. You may well fault advertising for its conservative ways, but when the winds of revolution are really blowing, the ad agencies are plugging in their fans.

ABSOLUT
The Metaphysics of Wrap

17

"ABSOLUT LARCENY" is the second part of a twin ad run on two consecutive right-hand pages. You don't need to have seen the companion ad in order to recognize the product, even if it's not there. Nor do you need to be able to read English in order to understand what's gone on. All you need to see is the backlit halo, the two-word format, and the broken chain. You fill in the missing product *as well as* the previous ad and the seemingly never-ending campaign.

For those who don't remember, the previous ad showed the Absolut bottle wrapped in chains over the blocked words "Absolut Security." I'll admit this is not one of the better twosomes (remember "Absolut Magnetism," in which the bottle seems to be pulling words across the spine toward the bottle on the right-hand side, or "Absolut Peppar," in which the heat of the flavored vodka pictured on the left has burned the outline of the bottle on the next page?), but it'll do, just as reading the not-very-sophisticated *Timon of Athens* may be a rewarding way to approach Shakespeare's more elaborate works. And, as chefs say, what is sent back to the kitchen is often more important than what is eaten.

Flops tell lots. This campaign has been so successful that in less than twenty years almost everyone can decode this ad and imagine the missing one. Even more intriguing is that this recall (according to Ad Track, this campaign ranks at the top for all print ads) has been achieved primarily by using only one medium—glossy magazines—and in only one format—two-word copy (really only one-word copy, since the first word is always Absolut).

Absolut Larceny was shown on a right-hand page following Absolut Security (the bottle in chains) in the 1980s.

So why the success? What makes these images so popular that not only do they end up in museums and downloaded from Web sites, but the company even sells them in a three-disk software package titled "Absolut Museum"? Talk about the reconfigured canon!

Even more interesting to students of popular culture is that these ads become objects of value to kid collectors who trade them like baseball cards. Librarians have routinely found Absolut ads razored out of magazines, so they have even marked up the ads to make them worthless to trade. Absolut Larceny larceny.

Although the politically correct may claim that children are attracted to the forbidden product, such does not seem the case. The kids are pulled in by the ads themselves—just like the rest of us.

In fact, magazines themselves clamor to carry tailor-made ads, even allowing their own vaunted editorial integrity to be compromised. *Harper's* okayed its trademarked Harper's Index to be enclosed in an Absolut bottle; *Artforum* magazine has run an Absolut ad on its inside back cover while on the facing page it has run a list of contemporary art exhibitions under the heading "Absolut Art"; *Playboy* featured a foldout Absolut bottle (Absolut Centerfold—naked of all "trade dress") complete with standard bio and vital statistics; *The New Yorker* rented out its cartoonists for special ads; and *New York* magazine has for years restructured its Christmas issue in order to carry one of Absolut's "extravaganzas."

The pull of Absolut's magnetic advertising is curious because the product itself is so bland. Vodka is aquavit, and aquavit is the most unsophisticated of alcohols. It is for novices and experts—you either put something in it to give it taste, or you drink it down because you don't want to taste it. No taste, no smell. You don't savor aquavit; there are no vodka connoisseurs, no vodka sampling parties. In other words, the taste is not *in* the product.

In fact, the Swedes, who make the stuff, rarely drink Absolut. They prefer cheaper brands such as Explorer, Renat Brannwinn, or Skane. That's because Absolut can't advertise in Sweden, where alcohol advertising is against the law.

The taste is clearly in the packaging and the semiotics that surround it. Thomas Hine, architecture critic and author of *The Total Package*, captures the conundrum when he repeatedly claims that packages understand people much better than people understand packages. For clearly what we are drinking is the container, not the mashed wheat and potatoes. As I've said, the same goes for many products: the more bland and unindividualistic the product, the better the advertising must be to sell it. And often, as with cigarettes, beer, and other like products, this is where you find cutting-edge advertisements.

Start with Absolut's bottle. There is a saying in advertising that if you can sell the product, then sell the product. But if you can't, then sell the package. You sell what has been called, since the eighteenth century, the trade dress. Ironically, it is as hard to sell alcoholic spirits with no smell as it is to sell aromatic liquids with lots of smell. That's why vodka companies have learned so much from the perfumeries.

Cruise the perfume aisle of your local drugstore and what do you see? Fragrance comes to us from the land of the surreal, literally contained in the absurd. It comes in bottles shaped like a hat pretending to be a shoe, inside tiny apples, mummy cases, molded elephants, African statues, and skyscrapers of aqua-colored glass. Ouvrez Moi is in a black glass handbag. Cut-glass crystal must somehow be made to express the mood and personality of the fragrance inside. Sometimes bottle designers get their inspiration from the fragrance's name: Poison comes in a sinister little flask. Gravity, advertised as having "the magnetism to pull men and women together," is in a bottle that appears to lean, as if succumbing to the force of gravity. And so on.

At the top end of the perfume market, however, sculpture rules. Delettrez's Parfum XXIII was designed as a row of small, round bottles arranged to look like a string of graduated pearls. The Rosine scent bottles of the Paris couturier Paul Poiret were boldly enameled with stylized flowers that recalled the work of the Scottish Arts and Crafts designer Charles Rennie Mackintosh. Merle Norman, the American perfumer, put Adoration inside a golden Thai-style goddess whose impassive head popped off to reveal a faceted stopper.

Such bottles are so beautifully crafted that art museums, including New York's Metropolitan Museum and Museum of Modern Art, collect them as works of art. Indeed, flaconnage is an art form, and a costly one at that—a new design may easily run over a million dollars.

Now look at the Absolut bottle as perfume flaconnage on steroids. No one reads the calligraphy on the bottle below the brand name (read it sometime; it's ridiculous and has nothing to do with ingredients but everything to do with the practiced ease of what Castiglione called *sprezzatura*), but they do notice the name in blue block letters. *Absolut* comes from the original *Absolut Renat,* which means "absolutely pure," referring to the multiple distillation process called rectification, which removes the usual scumular impurities of the fermented potato. The bottle announces this purity not only in its form, but also from the fact that the entire label is literally inscribed *in* the glass. You have to see through it.

Purity of package form, purity of filtration, purity of brand name, even purity of place of manufacture (is there any place more pure than snowy Sweden?), as well as all that polite schoolgirl handwriting. Now put that under a halo and hang on tight. Things are getting religious again.

The halo has an interesting history. In the early Renaissance, the area around the head of a sacred character became a place to lay gold leaf, thereby showing *and* telling preciousness. This personage radiated value by literally emitting a *glory*. God was pictured in front of a sun-bursting triangle, Christ had a halo with a cross and circle (which still appears on Oreos!), saints had just a circle behind the head, the Virgin Mary had a corona of small stars, and so on.

Absolut Perfection,
1981.

Of course, in artspeak you can't refer to this glory as a halo; it is formally called a nimbus. It might be noted in passing that at just about the same time that churchmen were having nimbi retrofitted into church art, secular leaders were having themselves fitted for gold crowns.

Although Absolut now gets the searchlight halo, the campaign started with a literal light circle (a late Renaissance development of a halo on the cheap—just white paint, no gold) hovering over the bottle's neck. According to Richard Lewis, executive vice-president and group account director at TBWA, who has chronicled this campaign in *Absolut Book*, this halo was conceived on a November evening in 1980, soon after TBWA Advertising landed the account. Geoff Hayes, an art director at the agency, doodled a halo over the bottle of Absolut. Then he added these words: "Absolut. It's the perfect vodka." Next morning he showed it to Graham Turner, a copywriter, who suggested shortening the headline to "Absolut Perfection."

The hard part was over. You can't make a package more heroic than this. It has for purity what Coke's Mae West bottle has for sensuousness or Nabisco's inner seal has for security. Now the task was to control the desire to be creative and thereby muck it up. TBWA and Michel Roux, president/CEO of Carillon Importers, succeeded. They never tested with focus groups, they never did any research, they almost never experimented. To be sure, there were those Christmas extravaganzas like the ad containing a computer chip that played Christmas carols when you turned the page, the ad that mimicked a snow globe, and another that featured 309 tiny red and green magnets to spell out sentences on the fridge, but such follies were more a sign of confidence than of marketing.

TBWA and Roux just kept, as N. W. Ayer used to say, everlastingly at it—some 600 ads' worth. In so doing they continually borrowed interest and value from such disparate places as cities and states ("Absolut D.C." has the bottle wrapped in red tape), designer fashion (the label made into a garment), cartoons (especially from *The New Yorker*), highcult concerns ("absolut cummings" has all label text lowercased), and so on.

Certainly the best known Absolut association has been with Pop art. After all, this is an art director's campaign in which image does all the heavy lifting, so who best to employ but other artisans? And, after all, isn't this the legacy of Thomas J. Barratt, whose genius was in realizing that engraving *Pears* on the bar of soap in a corner of a painting not just

Absolut Warhol, 1985.

changed the title from *A Child's World* to *Bubbles*, but also changed the entire meaning of the image? So when Richard Lewis tells the tale of how Andy Warhol "proposed painting his own interpretation of the Absolut Vodka bottle, and Michel [Roux] agreed, not even considering its use in advertising, but merely thinking, Let's see what happens" (Lewis 1996, 65), we might pause to contemplate that things might have been a bit more complex on both sides of the transaction.

No matter, Mr. Roux got more value back than the $65,000 he paid Warhol for the famous "black" Absolut bottle with the yellow halo now behind the bottle's shoulders. He got all Pop art—Ed Ruscha, Keith Haring, and Kenny Scharf. What a propitious con-

nection! Has any art movement been more in love with packaging than Pop, any group more fascinated with containers, any generation more venerative toward advertising, or any more willing to lend a hand? This is the ultimate synergy: both sides increasing their value.

All this iconizing of the object, however, is not without danger. Remember the Golden Calf? Iconoclasm, or the destruction of mythic value, is always a threat. The ads are always just on the edge of self-parody anyway; it doesn't take much to push them over. Although Absolut parodies are all over the Web, the most on-target series has come from north of the border, from Adbusters, a Canadian anticommercialism group. They ran a parodic series in their magazine of the same name, which included such entries as a hangman's noose in the bottle's contour over the line "Absolute Hangover," and one of a coffin in the Absolut silhouette reading "Absolute Nonsense." The ad went on to state: "Any suggestion that our advertising campaign has contributed to alcoholism, drunk driving or wife and child beating is absolute nonsense. No one pays any attention to advertising." Absolut lawyers threatened suit. Adbusters added the final "e" to the brand name and, in a press release, challenged the vodka company to a public debate on the pros and cons of alcohol advertising. Absolut lawyers in absolut retreat.

But if the Absolut campaign shows anything, it is that the ancient yearning for objects of value has continued unabated. Harness this yearning and you can load value into an interchangeable product. Certainly an increase of sales some 14,000 percent in fifteen years counts for something, certainly the fact that Absolut is the best-selling imported vodka, and certainly the fact that this bottle is now recognized almost as quickly as the golden arches says something. Even Smirnoff paid Absolut the ultimate tribute by archly admitting the obvious—sometimes superficiality can be deep.

But if you really want to see mute but eloquent testament to the Absolut icon, go to the liquor store and cruise the premium vodka aisle. There they are, the patient wannabes hoping for their breakthrough campaign: Finlandia's highly sculptural bottle looks just like Ittala crystal; Fris (complete with umlauts) resembles the Citigroup building; a brand called Icy is clearly knocking off Absolut's label-as-bottle format; Belvedere, Chopin, and Grey Goose all achieve 3D effects with etched images on the inside back surfaces of the bottle that shimmer through the front label, and Skyy is in a sky-blue bottle looking just like something you might have found on Granny's bedside table. Compare the contents and you will see why they need these elaborate delivery systems, the trade dress, packaged absolutly.

APPLE'S *1984*

The Ad as Artifact

A FEW YEARS AGO, in a tenderhearted and well-meaning way, an English professor at the University of Virginia, E. D. Hirsch, published a book called *Cultural Literacy*. It had the daunting subtitle *What Every American Needs to Know*. The thesis was compelling. If we want to unite as a nation, we first need to share a culture. From a white-bread professor at a white-bread university one could guess that the cultural matrix he would prescribe would be white-bred. In fact, Hirsch's prescription for the body politic was the ingestion of massive doses of the Dead White Male culture.

Many minority groups were predictably outraged—perhaps with reason—for what follows is the kind of information the professor thought necessary for social binding. I made this list by choosing the lower right-hand entries from each page in the appendix, cleverly titled "What Literate Americans Know."

ampersand	Auschwitz	biochemical pathways
Bundestag	Neville Chamberlain	complex sentence
cyclotron	dog in the manger	Elysian Fields
federalism	Indira Gandhi	D. W. Griffith
Hoover Dam	installment buying	Joseph and his brothers
Leibnitz	Ferdinand Magellan	Herman Melville
National Guard	nucleotide	paradox
planets	prosecution	Reign of Terror
sacred cow	Shawnee Indians	Battle of Stalingrad
taproot	topsoil	vector
Winnie the Pooh	Richard Wright	Zurich

Now take this list into any university in the country. Ask students how much they know about what they *ought* to know. Maybe they know half. Now give them *this* list and see how they do.

Just do it	Uh-huh	Colonel Sanders
Morris	Feel really clean	Heartbeat of America
Mmmm Mmmm good	Kills bugs dead	Mrs. Olsen
Fahrvergnügen	Quality is job 1	Why ask why?
Two scoops!	Because I'm worth it	Tony the Tiger
Have it your way	99⁴⁴⁄₁₀₀%	Master the moment
57 Varieties	Speedy	Never had it, never will
White Knight	Jolly Green Giant	Mountain grown
Mr. Whipple	Do you know me?	Be all that you can be
Betty Crocker	Still going	Snap, Crackle, Pop
Aunt Jemima	We try harder	That's Italian

Clearly something terrible has happened. They know almost every entry, even though much of this information predates their birth. And more interesting still, they all seem to know about the same amount. Blacks and whites, males and females, front row and back row, do have a common culture.

But advertising? That's our culture? Of course we are embarrassed by this. That what we share is a taste not for epicurian delights but for cultural junk food is so ... unappetizing. It has no taste, no calories. There is nothing behind this knowledge, no historical or cultural event, no reason to know it other than how to behave in the checkout line.

Yet it is precisely the recognition of jingles and brand names, precisely what high-culturists abhor, that does indeed hold us together. We may not know what is in the solar system, but we know what's in a Big Mac.

To appreciate this rich irony, let's go one step further. On page 193 of Hirsch's appendix is this entry: George Orwell. Presumably we should know Mr. Orwell because he wrote the dystopian masterpiece *1984*. A generation ago, the mere mention of the date rattled all who heard it. It should have. For here was a book to conjure with. Here was a book that was not just a political allegory of the modern state, but also a guide to the symbols of modern life.

In *1984*, all nations are in perpetual war. The Party, run by Big Brother, sees to it that there is no peace. Should any of the proles (proletariat) step out of line and slap "Question Authority" stickers on the bumpers of their scootermobiles, they are soon visited by the Thought Police. Political conformity crushes all individuality. And how are these aberrant proles found out? They are perpetually observed via the microphone and the telescreen. By "doublethink" and the big lie, the Party continually rewrites history, continually rejiggers reality, until all strays are brought into conformity.

Advertising is omnipresent. Consumption deadens rebellion. And how does Orwell feel about advertising? In a phrase, here's his famous definition: "the rattling of a stick in a swill bucket."

It helps to know this to appreciate how Apple Computer introduced its Macintosh to the world. The Mac ad is called *1984;* it was shown only once, in 1984, and, paradoxically, it removed George Orwell's novel *1984* from the reservoir of cultural literacy.

Go back into that classroom of eighteen-year-olds and ask them for the meaning of "1984." Now, admittedly, the real meaning of 1984 was effaced on New Year's Day 1985, but the myth of Big Brother and the nefarious state was profoundly rewritten by sixty seconds in the third quarter of Super Bowl XVIII on January 22, 1984. Had you been watching, here's what you would have seen:

OPEN ON AN ORWELLIAN VISION OF THE FUTURE. MINDLESS,
HOLLOW-EYED PEOPLE MARCH IN LOCKSTEP TOWARD A HUGE
ASSEMBLY HALL, WHERE BIG BROTHER HARANGUES THEM WITH
THE PARTY LINE ON A HUGE VIDEO SCREEN.

BIG BROTHER: For today, we celebrate the first glorious anniversary of the Information Purification Directives. We have created, for the first time in all history...a garden of pure ideology...

AS THE CROWD STARES, UNSEEING, AT THE VIDEO SCREEN, AN ATHLETIC YOUNG WOMAN, PURSUED BY GUARDS, RUNS INTO THE HALL WIELDING A SLEDGEHAMMER.

BIG BROTHER:...Where each worker may bloom secure from the pests of contradictory and confusing truths. Our Unification of Thought is more powerful a weapon than any fleet or army on earth. We are one people. With one will. One resolve. One cause. Our enemies shall talk themselves to death. And we will bury them with their own confusion. We shall prevail!

THE WOMAN RUNS TOWARD THE SCREEN, WINDS UP AND THROWS THE SLEDGEHAMMER WITH ALL HER STRENGTH. THE SCREEN EXPLODES IN A BLINDING FLASH OF LIGHT WHICH SWEEPS OVER THE STARING, UNCOMPREHENDING CROWD.

ANNCR: On January 24th, Apple Computer will introduce Macintosh. And you'll see why 1984 won't be like "1984."

What this official text, provided by the agency, Chiat/Day, cannot do is to pay tribute to the concussive power of this scenario. In fact, I include the words because they are of almost no importance. Ask someone who has seen the ad and they usually say there is no spoken language in it at all. That's because the *mise-en-scène* is so striking.

The imagery was constructed by Ridley Scott, the director of *Alien* and *Blade Runner*. It is clear from the first image of drone humans shuffling in lockstep through what seems to be a transparent tube into the auditorium—a scene lifted from the Weimar

cinema of Murnau or Lang—that Mr. Scott has no interest whatsoever in making a commercial. None. He's clearly making a
movie, an homage to German Expressionism. This is not the work
of an adman on the take, but of an *auteur*!

As well, everything else in this commercial says it's not one.
Along with the blockbuster production values, the lingering
scenes of the openmouthed drones, the storm troopers with their
face masks, the big-screen portrayal of Big Brother with all the
superscript words passing around his face, the audio track that
picks up the young lady's breathing, and the pacing of the pursuit
into the auditorium are all the stuff of German cinema filtered
through Hollywood, not American commercialism filtered through
Madison Avenue.

But, of course, just as it's not an ad, it's *not* a movie. So it must
be something else, some other genre. In fact, *1984* is an event, or,
better yet, a pseudo-event.

Apple's cost-conscious board of directors certainly knew it was
no ad, and no movie. Whatever it was, they didn't want it. The
only symbolism they recognized was at the very end, in the last
seconds, as black-and-white scenario gives way to a color image of
the bitten Apple—knowledge consumed.

The board had some reason to be concerned. When the ad
was copy-tested for effectiveness, it received the lowest-ever score
for a business machine commercial: a net pre/post effectiveness
score of 5 against a norm of 29. The range for all commercials was
13 to 42. Worse still, the norm was for thirty-second spots, and
1984 was sixty seconds (Goldberg 1994, 21). So it made sense to
"can" it. They instructed the marketing staff and the agency to
cancel the ad and begin selling off the broadcast time—the 120
seconds (the ad was to run twice) had already been purchased.

Apple lore—probably apocryphal—holds that the company's
quiet founder, Steve Wozniak, who was then only minimally

involved, approached Steve Jobs, took out his checkbook, and said, "I'll pay for half if you pay for the other half."

And Chiat/Day lore holds that the agency did indeed sell one of the already purchased minutes to United Airlines and McDonald's, but insisted that the commercial run. Detractors say they would have sold off the other minute if only there had been takers. The agency already had quite a stake in this piece of film: they had spent $100,000 to make it and ponied up $500,000 for the sixty-second slot.

Worse still, if ever there was an event that was dated, here it was. The ad either ran in 1984 or it never ran. In fact, Chiat/Day's initial concern was that someone else would beat them to the date. They feared that a phone company, perhaps one of the Baby Bells, would use the Big Brother theme to hammer AT&T on the eve of its breakup.

No matter, creations of this magnitude always have more than enough parents. What is clear is that two days before the Super Bowl, Apple still owned the time, and the economics of the situation won out. The board grudgingly approved airing *1984*.

In retrospect, the question now becomes, if it's not an ad, and not a movie, how do we treat it? Clearly, with some confusion. For instance, *Advertising Age* considers it the Commercial of the Decade of the 1980s, and it won the top prize at the Cannes International Advertising Film Festival. But *Entertainment Weekly* did not anoint it as one of "the fifty greatest commercials of all time" (March 3, 1995): instead, they found it "just so pretentious." In fact, in a feature that accompanies their list, the Apple spot is deemed the "most overrated commercial" ever.

So let's just say it's an event, albeit a pretentious one. For it did something that advertising has since repeatedly attempted. It got talked about. A lot. And in so doing, it got into communal consciousness. It became part of cultural literacy for a generation that marked its milestones not by books read or movies seen, but by ads consumed.

First, of course, the spot announces not just the product but a way of using it. The Mac is positioned not as a machine but as a style, an approach. Remember the catchphrase "user-friendly"? Here is where it starts. Without mentioning the simple Motorola 6800 microprocessor, without mentioning the affordable price of $2,500, without claiming home as opposed to office use, without foregrounding the mouse, without showing a new graphic user interface using icons, the ad does it all by using gender.

The Mac is female. Conversely, IBM must be male. IBM is not just male, it is Big Brother male. And Apple is not just female, but New Female. She is strong, athletic, independent, and, most important, liberated. After all, that's what the young athlete is all about. She is, in terms of the 1980s, empowerment *and* freedom.

Freedom for all. This is not just women's liberation. It's for everyone. Recall that the other players in this vignette of modern times are males: all those slackjawed drones, all those once-powerful men made ciphers by the doublethink of Big Brother. Need I mention that the image being used by IBM to represent its take on modern life was Charlie Chaplin playing the Little Tramp? In fact, one of the most important impacts this ad had was on the programmers and graphic designers who wrote software. They were revolutionary players at Apple, subverters, not sold-out employees at Big Blue, company men.

Not only was this event able to layer itself *over* a canonical work of high culture, over the women's movement, over IBM's entire advertising campaign, even over the growing anti-big-government sentiment associated with the Reagan "revolution," it also layered itself *into* one of the central male institutions of modern life: the Super Bowl, or, as it has since become, the Advertising Bowl.

The Super Bowl is the sweat lodge of modern masculinity. Every January millions of males, looking rather like their compatriots from Apple's *1984*, slowly file into bars, living rooms, entertainment centers, and clubs to watch what is usually a predictably dull game. The football will be moved for about eighteen minutes. Yet the show takes three hours. A few years ago a record of sorts was set when 44 percent of a forty-five-minute stretch was dedicated to commercials and promos. This is not a game. It is a carnival of commercialism.

Best yet for advertisers, it has developed the almost perfect demographics for certain products like cars, beer, and computers. Roughly 40 percent of eighteen- to forty-nine-year-old males watch the event, and almost half of those list seeing the commercials as a reason they watch. An astonishing 7 percent say they watch *only* for the ads.

The flood of advertising moves through the game and out into culture. More ink is spilled covering the campaigns than the game. The upstart *USA Today* goes all out, having sixty-eight volunteers wired to the "admeter" to record second-by-second reactions to commercials. Even *The New York Times* and the *The Wall Street Journal* dedicate tons of newsprint to the Super Bowl ads. This is why commercial time on the Super Bowl is so expensive— averaging well over $1.6 million for thirty seconds. Here you break out of advertising and become ... an event.

The most important play in the Super Bowl is the launching of new campaigns, a legacy of this Apple ad. We know that companies making razors, colas, credit cards, beer, computers, athletic shoes, and automobiles will be showing us something new. We even know that the game will end when the Most Valuable Player says, "I'm going to Walt Disney World!" (for which he pockets $50,000 to $75,000). The next day the MVP often appears on a box of Wheaties. We know all this because, to paraphrase Yogi

Berra, the Super Bowl is déjà vu all over again. See it once, you've seen it a thousand times. Only the ads change. But they are all attempting the same thing: be like Mac, be hip, make news.

There is a downside to this, of course. What happens to advertising when it loses its grip on the product and becomes just another form of entertainment event is that it ceases to sell. Witness Nike, Energizer batteries, Nissan, Budweiser, Pepsi, Levi's, British Airways, to name only a few, and you will see the ineluctable influence of the advertising-made event. What you are selling is a sensation—Wow! Did You See That Ad?—an entertainment, and often that obfuscates what the product is and what it does.

Toward the end of the 1996 Clio Awards, after showcasing the year's most brilliant ads, emcee Bill Maher quipped, "Boy, if the shows were as good as these commercials, TV wouldn't suck so much." That may be good news for viewers, but it sends shivers up the spines of sponsors. After all, they want you to behave exactly like the drones portrayed in *1984*, quietly marching up to, and over the edge, of the buy-hole.

And, worse, once a pseudo-event has been etched into pseudo-cultural literacy, it is very hard to get it out. A year later, Chiat/Day returned to the scene of the crime with a new commercial updating *1984*. In *Lemmings*, which introduced Apple's Macintosh Office line of office automation products, we see another long line of drones, this time men and women dressed for success, who are wending their way up a hill. They are blindfolded. When they reach the top, each jumps off the edge of a cliff, representing businesspeople blindly following the leader. The last in line decides to pull off the blindfold as a disembodied voice says something about the Macintosh Office. Not only is this version hopeless—there is no resolution, as there was in *1984*—but the assumption—IBM is for brainwashed idiots—is simply insulting. *Lemmings* was such a disaster that it is one of the reasons Chiat/Day lost the Apple account the following year.

Still, the legacy of Apple's *1984* lives on—advertising as event. The idea that selling products has co-opted the traditional function of the liberal arts and is now defining the objects of common desire could have been expected. That it occasionally has been able to invest in these commercial objects the sense of the ineffable, the *mysterium terrendium,* might also have been predicted. After all, the purpose of a blockbuster event is generally to explode quickly into a lot of free publicity. Just like what? A book, a painting, a musical composition.

So why shouldn't our best talents be used in its employ? Ridley Scott was just one of the first to rent his imagination. When David Lynch makes ads for Calvin Klein's Obsession, using passages from D. H. Lawrence, Ernest Hemingway, and F. Scott Fitzgerald, the "aura" of art culture is subsumed by a commercial pseudo-event. When an artist like John Frankenheimer makes ads for AT&T, when Jean-Luc Godard is employed by a French jean company, when Woody Allen makes spots for Campari, when Spike Lee produces campaigns for Levi's, Nike, the Gap, and Barney's, the visionary imagination that had served the Church and the State is now serving Industry. When the entire fifth floor of the Centre Georges Pompidou in Paris is dedicated to the "Art of Advertising, 1890–1990," or when the Museum of Modern Art in New York sponsors a show called "The Art and Technique of the American Television Commercial," you know that advertising is no longer the culture of the Visigoths but the culture of Rome. It has become part of—gasp!—cultural literacy, maybe not What Every American *Needs to* Know, but, worse, What Every American *Does* Know.

THE RISE AND FALL AND RISE OF THE INFOMERCIAL

"Call Now! Operators Are Standing By . . ."

THE INFOMERCIAL is the Rodney Dangerfield of advertising. Treated with disrespect bordering on disdain, from night till morning this genre of advertising endlessly plays out its shtick before droopy-lidded viewers. What's it selling now? Worthless vitamin supplements, psychic friends, ways to quit smoking without using willpower, scalp paint that makes you look less bald but more ridiculous, how to get juice from a turnip, confidence radiation systems, kitchen knives that can cut rocks, a wax so tough that your car can resist a flamethrower?

Whatever it is, chances are that success is coming your way if you'll just call now. Money Back Guaranteed. Infomercials have given "As Seen on TV" a bad name, and have made the snake oil salesman at the carnival seem respectable in comparison.

The infomercial is advertising achieving transcendental form. If romantic art struggled for the condition of opera, and if Newtonian science aspired to pure mathematics, then television—all modern, free-market, commercial television—seeks the state of pure ad, a seamless web of entertaining by selling and selling by entertaining. Its most recent growth has been caused by many factors, none more so than the fact that the number of TV stations has ballooned and there is a lot of air to fill. Advertising no longer sponsors programming; it has *become* programming.

The infomercial is the fifteen-, thirty-, or sixty-second spot blown up to Brobdingnagian proportions, and as such it provides the eerie satisfaction of an adolescent poring over a blackhead viewed in a magnifying mirror lit by an arc lamp. If you want to

understand the complexion of electronic advertising, this is a good place to start looking.

While the television infomercial is recent, its ancestry is ancient, at least in advertising time. When Claude Hopkins had the genius in the 1930s to attach a coupon to a print ad and then sit back and wait for the mail, he was at last doing something *scientific* with advertising. He was tracing results, putting a needle on the dial of desire, turning the machine off and on. Hopkins would write a number of ads for a product, say Pepsodent toothpaste or Palmolive soap, then place these different ads in different versions of the same newspaper or magazine, each with a coded coupon. Usually the code was simple, just a different post office box. By collating the responses from this split-run, he could tell which ad "drew" best, and now he knew which version he should spend his money on.

The coupon in the infomercial is the 800 number. Little did AT&T know when they developed the WATS concept in 1968 that it would transform the act of interactive shopping. This number is Hopkins's coded box number. While you may think that the infomercial you are seeing at one-thirty in the morning is the same one seen by everyone else who cannot get to sleep (and some 15 percent of the people who own television sets are watching at that time!) such is not the case. The infomercial programmer is continually readjusting his pitch until he finds the point of harmonic convergence.

The other great innovation captured on this frozen television image—called a "tag" or "billboard" in the trade—is the credit card number. Quick, efficient, and ripe with yet more information (this time for the bank), the sixteen-digit number continues the circuit. "Sorry No CODs" appears not only because involving the post office is a nuisance, but also because anything that slows the connection between seeing the ad, calling the number, and paying for the product is wasted time. The distance between "you've got to have" and "yes, send me one" is thus nanosecond-quick, about the time of a synapse firing.

The circuit is finally completed by the telemarketer at the other end of the phone, usually in Utah, who receives your call, tabulates which infomercial you saw by the 800 or 888 number you called, notes the content of your call, and keyboards the results to the direct-marketing service. Since 75 to 95 percent of all calls are made within thirty minutes of the broadcast, the marketer can tell exactly how each version of the ad is pulling in each demographic part of the audience. The telemarketer may also attempt to up-market or cross-market your call by suggesting you buy more of a product (another box of vitamins, more videotapes) or a different product (a dietary supplement, audio tapes).

Rules of thumb: one out of every hundred people watching an infomercial for longer than fifteen minutes should call and purchase the product immediately or you will lose money; if more than half the calls are for more information, then there is a mistake inside the ad; if there is a sudden decrease in calls from a certain market, then the ad has started to "wobble" and needs to be replaced; if callers cannot be moved to other products, then the entire category may have become exhausted and deserves a rest. When an area is hot, as, say, the concept of rock-hard abdominals currently is, the market is very hard to glut. That's why you can sell the Ab Roller and Ab Sculptor, Ab Max and Ab Coach, Ab Ex, Ab Isolator, Portable Ab Roller, and Ab Roller Plus. No where else in Adland is this pot of merchandising gold buried.

So why was the infomercial so long in coming? Actually, if the government had kept its hands off the electronic media, the infomercial would have been a staple of radio and television broadcasting almost since day one. Early radio was filled with proto-infomercials, as individual ads had not been hurried out of programming to be bundled in their little pods. Popular belief to the contrary, the government never mandated the number or duration of commercials for each broadcast hour; the Federal Communications Commission merely suggested what they thought was appropriate. During the 1930s, the suggestion was that no more than seven minutes per hour be allocated for the sponsor. Modern television has doubled that number.

Before those "suggestions," in the radio soap operas for instance, it was quite common that a company like Pillsbury would include cooking instructions for its cake mixes right in the program. After all, in the early days the show itself was created by the advertising agencies. So, on Irna Phillips's groundbreaking *Today's Children*, Mother Moran, a trustworthy teacher if ever there was one, would try a product. While frosting a cake, she would explain to Lucy, her granddaughter, "I got the new kind of flapper that you can be icing the cake right on the platter." Or, later in the episode (August 8, 1933, episode 293), while admiring her finished product, she comments wistfully, "And to think that this cake is not one of my own recipes, but a recipe I took right off the flour box." The announcer would politely interrupt to tell her the product was now available at neighborhood stores. After a pause for the housewife to dutifully write down the necessary information, the action would recommence.

Mother Moran's descendants—Jay (the Juiceman) Kordich, Richard (Sweating to the Classics) Simmons, Tony (your "one-on-

one personal trainer") Little, Susan (Stop the Insanity) Powter, Victoria ("Principal Secret" skin care) Principal, Ron (Amazing Discoveries) Popeil, Suzanne (ThighMaster) Somers, and Tony (Thirty Days to Personal Power) Robbins—would be proud of her flawless technique of mixing selling with entertainment.

Alas, by the 1940s, the FCC was insisting that all such commercialism be separated from the programming, and since they controlled the licenses, it was. Jack Benny was encouraged to stop saying "Jell-O again" as a sign-on, and Arthur Godfrey was told to quit asking for more Lipton Tea during his show. But what the FCC rent asunder with radio, the more modern FCC put back together with television.

With the proliferation of cable stations and the possibility that stations would have overlapping programming, Mark Fowler, a Reagan appointee to the FCC (whose most famous pronouncement was that TV was "just another appliance—a toaster with pictures"), ruled in June 1984 that "commercial time restraints" could be lifted *under certain circumstances*. If your local station and a superstation, like WTBS from Atlanta, were showing reruns of *Gomer Pyle* at the same time, then the local station could program anything at all during that time slot. A break for the "little guy."

As you might imagine, the little guy soon hired sophisticated programmers who would slot shows precisely to be in conflict with another station. On the theory that one good investment was worth a lifetime of hard work, the local station, which was mandated by law to be carried on the cable, was now able to make some real money and could do it legally.

Problem was that there was simply no "long-form" programming to fit into these half-hour blocks. Surplus time, called "remnants" or "slag," was dirt-cheap because no one realized it was loaded with advertising ore.

No one, that is, but the toy companies. They understood another marketing concept: find a need and fill it quick. Companies like Hasbro and Mattel tied local stations together in a temporary network for certain times of the day when the kiddies were at home. Afternoon cable was soon filled with toy-based shows like *He-Man, GI Joe, Thundarr the Barbarian, Blackstar*, and *Mr. T*, in which plastic vigilantes literally pounded good sense and manners into evil villains. The progenitor of the modern bash-'em-up storm troopers is Prince Adam, a.k.a. He-Man, who, together with the Masters of the Universe, was continually at war protecting his natal Castle Grayskull from the evil Skeletor. His real job, however, was to sell toys.

In a merchandising coup, Filmation Associates, a subsidiary of Westinghouse, animated a fantasy around this five-and-a-half-inch warrior and tried to sell it to the networks. *He-Man and the Masters of the Universe* was a crude, poorly crafted cartoon, but it was a savvy infomercial. The networks, still cautious about the relationship between advertising and entertainment, passed.

However, hundreds of independent stations on the cable were desperate for "filler" shows to put into the local-access airtime before the profitable prime time began at 8:00 P.M. The number of independents had tripled between 1972 and 1980, and most of them were unable to afford the prices of afternoon syndicated reruns, which the majors ran primarily to cover these mid-afternoon doldrums. As opposed to print media, where pages may be added to increase space, in electronic media you *must* add programming to fill up time. You can go "blank" at 2:30 A.M., but never at 2:30 P.M.

These independents, through the prototype of what is now called "barter syndication," were paid by exchanging air time for programming. The station received the programming gratis and then sold part or all of the commercial time and pocketed the proceeds. By the time *Thundercats* came to the market in the mid-1980s, Lorimar Telepictures cut a deal whereby they paid a percentage return to the station that was based on how well the toys were selling in the broadcast area. To maximize its return, the television station saturated its audience with specific toy-driven cartoons. The more toys sold, the larger the station's cut. They carved a direct path from airwaves to shopping aisles. Others would follow and colonize other parts of the broadcast day.

One of the first was Jerry Wilson, a onetime used-airplane salesman and bodybuilder, who cobbled together an exercise "station" that he called the Soloflex. Realizing that late-night broadcast time was even cheaper than late afternoon, Wilson called some stations around the country, rented their blank airtime, and simply sent them the instructional videos that accompanied his equipment. For a few dollars, he added the billboard page that included the 800 number, and the price calculated in easy installments.

For a while in the 1980s, this Soloflex instructional video was the most often-shown infomercial in the country. Thousands of couch potatoes watched in awe as two godlike youngsters worked themselves into an almost sexual lather. Then they called the 800 number, and paid almost $2,000 (when all the easy payments had been made).

The Chinese Wall between advertising and programming crumbled almost overnight at night. Local stations had been joined by entire cable networks like the USA Network, Lifetime, EXPN, TNN, and A&E, which either shut down after midnight or relied on reruns. They too were desperate for filler.

Quick and easy to produce, infomercials soon looked so much like real programs that it was often only in the last few minutes that you realized that the *cine noir* that you were watching, which was making you feel afraid to go out on the street, was really trying to sell you a stun gun. Or that the instructional exercise show with the perky people was really trying to sell you a home gymnasium. Or that those pleasant celebrities chatting in the living room were huckstering vitamin supplements and were being paid by the volume of incoming orders.

Although only one in ten infomercials really succeeded, this was a bonanza for products that sold for over thirty dollars and cost under five dollars. Hit it big, and you could make millions. Think only of the juicer, really just a souped-up blender. In 1991, juicers went from a $10 million retail category to a $380 million one solely because of infomercials.

To succeed, however, the infomercial had to pretend it was something else, because the bane of all television advertising is the remote-control clicker. The infamous "rule of two-thirds" applies: two-thirds of all viewers surf as a matter of normal viewing, and two-thirds of all the surfers start surfing whenever *any* commercial comes on. In other words, the mere presence of a commercial caused the finger to itch. Surf's up! Programmers estimate that you only have about two to ten seconds to get them to lighten the finger pressure and come to shore.

So the infomercial is organized to paralyze the finger momentarily. Over the years, a formula has evolved. Here's how it works: The product should be mentioned at least three times per minute; the Call to Action (CTA) should appear at least three times (every eight to ten minutes), during which time the billboard graphic with the 800 number is flashed; enthusiasm must never fade; urgency must be maintained, often by adding more extras; the magical benefits must be clear; and always, always, always, there must be a money-back guarantee.

While the internal combustion of closing the sale must be carefully timed, the engine can be hidden in any number of places. What is this? we ask ourselves, moving past channels at the speed of finger force. Is it a talk show, an amazing-discovery show, a lecture, a mass rally, a game show, a documentary, a network news show? And who are all these excited people? It only rarely crosses our minds that *everyone* we are seeing on the stage and in the audience is being paid for showing their barely controllable excitement.

Here the infomercial plays a special role in providing employment for often over-the-hill celebrities. In the trade they are known as "channel stoppers" because our curiosity about them slows down the nervous finger. So we see Cher, E. G. Marshall, John Davidson, Robert Vaughn, Joseph Campanella, Monty Hall, John Ritter, Chuck Norris, and Christie Brinkley enthusing us on to shell out $39.95 for hair cream, $297 for real-estate hints, $69.95 for no more smoking, $59.95 for a food substitute, or $248.95 for a little trolley that moves up and down along an inclined plane. We cannot easily pass by Barbi Benton assuring us that we can "Play the Piano Overnight"; Dick Clark answering the question "Is There Love after Marriage?"; Fran Tarkenton helping with "Personal Power, 30 Days to Unlimited Success"; Jane Fonda "walking to the music and making it burn" on a treadmill; and Brenda Vacarro letting us in on how to "Light His Fire."

Usually there is nothing particularly objectionable about these infomercials other than that they are being passed off as documentaries or spontaneous talk shows. If you are willing to sell time to Oral Roberts or to He-Man and the Masters of the Universe, whom can you deny? Anyone with a fistful of dollars can get on the "public airwaves."

Not only do stations get rid of excess time, they are also not liable as transmitters of deceptive ads. The worst that can happen is that the Federal Trade Commission can file a fraudulent-advertising complaint against the sponsor if enough viewers complain. Best yet, in the hallowed tradition of what transformed newspapers, the stations get paid up front.

Now that infomercials have stopped growing like algae at the edges of the programming pond, they are floating into prime time. To make the transition, they are being called "long-form marketing" and "direct-response television" (DRTV) instead. No longer are they butts of satire. (Remember the great "Bass-O-Matic" skit by *Saturday Night Live* comedian Dan Aykroyd, who dissolved a fish in a blender while shouting his sales pitch for the machine à la the hyperkinetic Ron Popeil?) They are attracting a loftier class of sponsors—companies like Volvo, Cuisinart, Sears, MCI, Saturn, Corning, Philips, and Apple Computer. This genre is no longer a "shout and pout, withhold and thrust" kind of selling, but a decorous way for companies to make an extended point, much the way the famous "hands" ads for Kraft introduced new products like Cheese Whiz to the market. You can show your audience how to use your product.

The influence of the infomercial should not be minimized. Not only has it spawned a print relative, the "advertorial" (the exploded advertising section that acts as a roadblock to reading, yet looks just like the surrounding text) and the "outsert" (the ad section that is "bagged" with the magazine, often prepared in the same editorial manner as the mother text), and not only are there at least two cable channels that just run infomercials—Product Information Network (PIN) and Advertising Television (ATV)— but the infomercial is the ontological basis of MTV (what are music videos but infomercials for tapes and CDs?) as well as the home-shopping networks and interactive buying on the World Wide Web.

What's next for the infomercial on television? The networks are currently contemplating showing an 800 number during the closing credits of a show announcing, say, that if you liked the trendy sofa you just saw on *Friends*, or the comfy sweater worn by Tim Allen on *Home Improvement*, it can be yours in easy payments. Call now! The industry even has a new coinage to describe the process of mutating the infomercial: it's called the direct-transaction business. They project that it may make up 5 percent of the network revenues by early next century. Keep your credit card next to the remote control, operators are standing ... buy.

NIKE AND MICHAEL JORDAN

The Hero as Product

WHAT YOU SEE before you is the Holy Grail of modern advertising: the synergy of two "power brands" woven together in flight. Not by happenstance does this image occur in an area where few of us spend much time—about five feet over our heads. We know who he is and why he is up there. Michael Jordan is not just the most recognized athlete in the world, he is the most recognized pitchman on the planet. We are at his feet not just because it puts the shoes at eye level, but because he performs a central oxymoron of our times—he is a man who flies.

In art-historical terms, Mr. Jordan is hanging there in the *sublime*—just below (*sub-*) the edge (*-limen*) of the next world. This is the literal Air Jordan. If you look at Renaissance church painting, or Impressionistic landscape painting, you realize that whatever is in this ethereal band of air is graced with transcendental meaning. The golden halo of a hovering Giotto angel, or the bursting sunlight at the horizon of a Turner vortex, is a signifer of man's ancient yearning for life above the *limen,* at the edge of transcendence. We want up and out of the dreary world of earth, and never tire of picturing it. We dream of soaring like a bird, not burrowing like a mole. Heaven is above us, hell the other way.

This mythography is not to detract from the exceptional athleticism of Mr. Jordan or the exceptional marketing of Weiden & Kennedy, the advertising agency who generated the leitmotif image, but only to point out the obvious. The up-jumping human goes deep, deep into the imagination. Naturally, whatever provides liftoff is ripe with magical meaning, even if it is just a smelly sneaker.

A jumping man becomes the Jumpman logo: The Michael Jordan campaign for Nike, 1980s to 1990s.

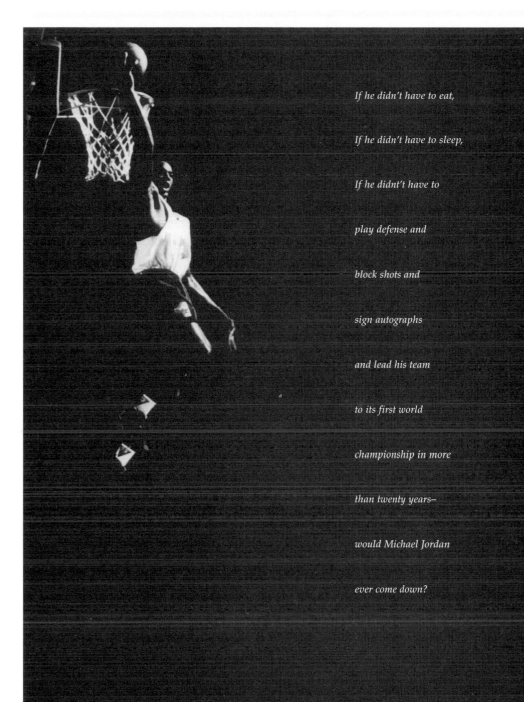

If he didn't have to eat,

If he didn't have to sleep,

If he didn't have to

play defense and

block shots and

sign autographs

and lead his team

to its first world

championship in more

than twenty years—

would Michael Jordan

ever come down?

When Michael Jordan defies gravity he wears Air Jordan® shoes with Nike Air® cushioning to absorb shock.

As a child I remember being entranced by the coiled-spring shoes advertised in *Boy's Life* magazine. In the cartoon that made up the ad, you saw a fellow kid bounding around like a kangaroo. You supposedly slid your shoes into a harness that was welded onto what looked like bed springs. And who was my favorite cartoon character at the same time? Superman, of course. He wore red boots. Superman was far more exciting than Batman, who couldn't jump into the air but had to spend most of his time swinging from ropes. And who was my favorite classical hero? Mercury, the winged god. Where did he get his swoosh? From those little winged sneakers.

Teenage boys want to leave the ground. Could becoming airborne be the reason why basketball is so powerful an attraction to adolescent males? Basketball players wear almost nothing but sneakers. No other athlete is so nearly naked and so completely birdlike. Pole vaulters come close. Go into any Niketown, as the retail outlets are called, and you will see images of Mr. Jordan bounding around the area just below the ceilings, and being flashed on the screens above your head. For a while his image was hovering, literally, over Times Square.

For ten years, Nike and Michael Jordan colonized this fly space. Although both have now come back to earth, how they ascended is one of the success stories of modern celebrity marketing. And it is also, if you listen to their vociferous detractors, the cause of much that is wrong with modern-day sport.

Fast-reverse back to television ads of the 1980s, and you will see how these two brands came together. In the spring of 1985, millions of prime-time television viewers saw a basketball roll quickly across an urban court toward a handsome kid at the edge of the tarmac. He easily caught the ball with the toe of one of his Technicolor shoes. He flipped it into his hands. Then he began to move across the blacktop to the whorling sound of jet engines revving to takeoff. By the time the engines reached critical scream, he was aloft, arms and legs splayed in a slow-motion tableau so magically vivid and elongated that it seemed he was waiting for us to climb aboard.

Michael Jordan stayed in the air with his legs apart for the last ten seconds of the commercial (and essentially for the rest of the eighties), fusing spectators who had never been to a basketball game with the abiding fantasy of athletic virtuosity and escape. The illusion was not just that he could fly like a bird, but that his wings were somehow laced around his feet, attached to bits of spongy rubber often surrounding pockets of trapped air.

The Nike commercial, *Jordan Flight,* was replayed so often that Michael Jordan became ever more famous as Air Jordan, the guy who could fly. So in another commercial, the sequence played out with not a word spoken until the phrase "Who said man wasn't meant to fly?" was flashed onto the screen.

Over and over we saw Mr. Jordan make the flight back to his customary perch five feet above our heads. Sometimes he went even higher. In one of the best-remembered television versions, he is seen entering a darkened warehouse, where he finds a 100-foot-high basketball hoop looming in the distance. After the requisite close-up of the shoes, he seems to accept some mysterious challenge from afar. He starts dribbling toward the hoop. Faster and faster. Cue the jet engines, because he now lifts off, soaring for a two-handed slam-dunk. Nothing but the swoosh of passing the sound barrier. But wait! The last frame has him hanging from the rim with a quizzical "Okay, now what do I do?" look as the perspective shifts back to far away. We see the basketball slowly falling forever to the ground.

Jordan, realizing his predicament and realizing that we've seen all this countless times before, flashes his patented smirk as we cut to the "Just Do It" slogan. The spot ends with a still-more-distant shot of him hanging from the hoop, our modern Icarus caught too close to the metal hoop of dreams.

Not only did this sequence of man merging with the Beyond form the promise of his requisite instructional video—*Come Fly with Me*—as well as the title of one of his biographies—*Taking to the Air*—it was at the center of his merging into Hollywood fantasy. In a blockbuster movie of the early nineties, *Space Jam*, Jordan joins forces with Bugs Bunny and his Looney Tunes pals to play a team of evil outer-space meanies in a basketball battle worthy of Ulysses and the Lestrygonians. If the whole movie looks just like a commercial, it should, since it was directed by the same man who oversaw many of the Nike spots, Joe Pytka.

His Airness, as Jordan is now openly called, saves the Looney Tunes characters by achieving his standard cruising lay-up altitude and then, thanks to his affiliation with animation, extends his Silly Putty arms over the galactic giants to achieve a dunk now worthy of Spider-Man. It is hard to watch this movie and not be aware that Jordan is being carefully fashioned as a modern icon whose job is not just to drop a basketball down a net, but to draw youthful consumers down the buy-hole of countless products.

As befits a consumerist parable, all versions of the tale essentially negotiate the same territory leading to the apocalyptic cash register. By the 1990s the *bricolage*, or interpenetration of various renditions, was so thick that independent authorship was impossible to determine. What remains in all the renditions is the incessant drumbeat of fly, fly, fly and buy, buy, buy.

As the sequence was mercilessly cloned by Nike, it was woefully misunderstood by its competitor, who tried to subvert it. Reebok, who played Pepsi to Nike's Coke, played the scenario upside down in an infamous bungee-jumping commercial. A jumping-down competitor comes out of his ill-fitting Nikes while the Reebok stays firmly attached. In the patois of the day, Reebok "just didn't get it." Nikes go up; no one cares about what happens when they go down.

As Spike Lee, speaking as fanboy Mars Blackmun, says at the conclusion of one of his versions of the Nike/Jordan campaign, "It's gotta be the shoes." Many youngsters believed him. For almost a generation, a nationwide Air Jordan basketball shoe-shopping spree ensued, replete with long lines, hoarding, kids cutting classes, a retail price as far above production costs as Mr. Jordan could jump (cost to produce, $5.50; selling price, $140), secondary street markets, traumatic disappointments over the limited supply, apocryphal tales of kids committing murder to own a pair, and the general aura of a buying panic. Before the brown-shoe backlash, Nike achieved the dubious distinction of being linked with illicit drugs (sneakers to kill for) and capitalism at its worst (sneakers made from the sweat of Asian women and kids). The once-smelly high-top was achieving the status of a marijuana cigarette and a bar of gold. The swoosh logo became the swoostika.

Just as Jordan and his shoes seemed to merge into a seamless myth of "getting free," so too did Nike and its advertising agency, Weiden & Kennedy. On Nike's side was Phil Knight, an eccentric, introverted, suspicious Stanford MBA who first sold Japanese shoes out of his car trunk and vowed, along with Bill Bowerman, University of Oregon track coach, never to sell out. That is, until they learned how to make a waffle-soled version that provided serious runners cushioned support.

On the agency side was Dan Weiden, whose independent spirit and often curmudgeonly manner made him a perfect foil. He knew that Knight's antiselling attitude—an attitude of grit, determination, and passion—was the perfect selling technique. His job was to link these traits to a slab of rubber, leather uppers, and some string, and make them mythic.

As both companies grew, they interpollinated. In fact, if you visit them—characteristically they are both at what is left of the

American frontier in Portland, Oregon—you will see that they are both commercial cults. While other companies have field technical representatives, Nike has Ekins (Nike spelled backwards). Ekins are passionate even to the point that many have the Nike logo tattooed on a thigh, where it shows with every stride when they run. Ditto Weiden & Kennedy, which has taken the "us against them" style of post-Bernbach advertising to a new level. They behave like artists, or at least the Hollywood version of artists. Stomping out in disgust is not just a sign of integrity, it's a way of doing business.

Visit their respective corporate headquarters and you see how similar the companies have become. As befits the modern corporation that stitches its logo on products made elsewhere, Nike looks like a combination of college campus and penitentiary. It is dug in. The buildings are named for the icons it has created; Knight's office is in the John McEnroe Building, preschoolers are dropped off in the Joe Paterno day-care facility, grownups work out at the Bo Jackson sports center. Whatever this is, it is *not* a shoe factory.

Go into W&K's Portland office and here's what you see: a gentrified turn-of-the-century downtown building with a center column of open space. When you enter the lobby, you see photos of everyone at the agency instead of the usual glass case of self-important awards. Above you are floors of offices, few with closed doors, and no titles. There is plenty of commotion, not the hushed, pinstriped calm of a big-time agency. On one floor is a small-version basketball court. W&K has no personnel department, no dress code, employee lists are alphabetized by first names, not rank, titles are left off business cards—it's all a little contrived, to be sure. But the point is that this is *not* an advertising agency. Dan Weiden proudly says it is patterned after a slime mold.

In retrospect, how interesting that Phil Knight's first comment to Dan Weiden in 1980 was, "I'm Phil Knight, and I hate advertising." He has since learned otherwise. He has come to realize that what Nike sells *is* advertising, that the advertising is the brand, and that the shoe is a by-product. One of Nike's most famous early ads was just a simple picture with a single line, "There is no finish line." The real finish line in the shoe business, however, is always at the same place: in front of the cash register.

Knight has come to understand a selling principle as old as tribal culture and as modern as Yogi Berra holding up a chocolate beverage and saying, "I'm for Yoo-Hoo." The concept is the magical—nay, mystical—power of endorsement. Endorsement depends on a peculiarly human phenomenon called "spontaneous trait transference." STT was the basis of the first great industry of Western man, an industry every bit as sophisticated as anything attempted by Madison Avenue—the merchandising of relics in the Middle Ages. Entire cathedrals were constructed around a reliquary in which a shard of holiness such as a knucklebone of a saint, a sliver from the True Cross, or the hair of the Redeemer lay in protective repose. Who cared if the provenance was dubious? For believers, the fact that the Shroud of Turin may be a fake only redoubles their enthusiasm. Overwhelming logic by fervent belief is the secret to the power of endorsement.

The desire to be close to our "betters" is at the heart of the "by appointment to the crown" trademarks on objects, why movie stars were forever puffing on cigarettes and washing with soap in the magazine ads of the 1940s, and why our president spends almost an hour of each day being photographed with well-wishers. What marks our current crop of endorsers is that they come to us from sporting events, especially those that can be televised.

What Weiden (and Jim Riswold, the account manager) showed Knight is that you can supercharge the endorsement process if you hype *not* the product, but the endorsing athlete. Face it, the shoe doesn't have a personality, the athlete does. Better yet—as opposed to royalty, movie stars, and politicians—most of them haven't been typecast, or at least not yet. Quite the opposite. For years the athlete has focused on doing a repetitive action perhaps to compensate for not having a confident and distinct sense of self.

In its Nike campaigns, W&K rewrote two of the most revered advertising adages of Adland: if you have nothing to say, have a celebrity say it; and you should always present the product as hero. Not only did Weiden make jocks articulate, he made them coherent personae. So you don't say that Bo Jackson uses your shoes. You say Bo is a super athlete. He knows far more than you ever will about sports, all sports. You show him playing baseball, football, tennis, hockey, and other sports leading up to the punchline of seeing him fumbling on the guitar. "Bo, you don't know diddly," says the real Bo Diddley, but the point remains. If he knows sports, all sports, he must know shoes—especially the cross-trainer. But the commercial never says that—it doesn't have to. We draw the inference as surely as our ancestors knew that any reliquary decorated in precious stones and covered by soaring arches housed the real object of holiness.

To give the athlete an oversized personality so he can be "read" quickly, you have to make him into something peculiarly ancient *and* modern. He needs to become celebrated. In all cultures certain people are capable of *celebratus,* or the condition of being honored, not just for what they have done, but for what they can continue to do for us. This recognition is not always a function of the individual's specific acts, but of the role he plays. In fact, the elevation of certain people—celebrities—is often dependent only on their being able to perform certain rites. In the church we still honor the role of the priest in "celebrating" certain events like baptism, the Eucharist, marriage, or the rites of death. The celebrity is that leader; he is the priest. Today we confer priestly status on actual people in the here and now. Celebrity is a point-of-sale, on-the-court phenomenon—a fleeting image en route to the checkout line; *sellebrity* would be a better spelling.

Clive James has pointed out in his book *Fame in the Twentieth Century* that people used to be famous for what they did. Then, he argues, in the modern world they became famous for what they were doing while they did what made them famous. I would argue that since the 1960s you are not known for what you did, or what you were doing when you did it. You are famous for what you endorse while doing what you did that used to be what made you famous. That is one reason why we are continually told how much the endorser is making to shill the product. We now think that if a Michael Jordan is using the product *and* if he is being paid outrageous sums to do it, then, ipso facto, the manufacturer *must* be making something really good. In other words, the value is not just flowing from endorser to product, but from product back to endorser. We have become accustomed not just to mistake value of object for value of the endorser, but to mistake value of the endorsement for the value of the object.

In a universe of interchangeable products, the celebrity endorsement has become a central part of commercial magic. "Be Like Mike," the Gatorade slogan promises. If you replenish your lost bodily fluids with their greenish liquid, you will not only be drinking Mr. Jordan's brand but will be participating in his majesty. This is what we have for the Eucharist. Jump like Mike, says Nike. Then go out and buy Michael Jordan cologne, created by the designer Bijan, slide into Hanes' Michael Jordan underwear, and cover up with his own Jumpman outerwear.

The ability to generate celebrity value and then quickly link that value to a product is not as easy as it seems, however. Sometimes the process can implode. Latrell Sprewell chokes his coach and the Converse shoe company gags. Remember the stink caused in the Barcelona Olympics when professional American basketball players, who were on the Nike payroll (and who, as professionals, had no business being there in the first place), almost refused to accept their gold medals while wearing sweatsuits emblazoned with a tiny Reebok logo. Let Michael Jordan experience the debacle of Michael Jackson and the poles of charismatic attraction can be reversed. While it was acceptable that Jordan bet huge sums (over $100,000) on golf and cards, let him bet on a basketball game and he will join Pete Rose in celebrity limbo.

Backsliding happens all the time as endorsers bounce checks on their cultural capital. Bruce Willis pitched Seagram's Golden Wine Cooler until it was rumored in tabloids that he had "a drinking problem." Once Mike Tyson and Robin Givens stopped cooing and started punching, Diet Pepsi headed for the showers. When Macaulay Culkin, star of the *Home Alone* movies, said of Sprite, "I'm not crazy about the stuff. But money is money," admen reached for the bourbon. James Garner underwent heart surgery and the beef industry bled. When Cybill Shepherd, spokeswoman for L'Oreal, admitted she didn't dye her hair, many admen pulled theirs. Need I even mention what happened to the relationship between Hertz and O.J. Simpson?

There are ways around the problem of celebrity crash. There is safety in numbers, which is why Nike, Reebok, Adidas, and Fila sign up a roster of athletes one month and then discharge them the next. (Or you can do what New Balance and K-Swiss do by claiming that they are "Endorsed by No One.") For the risk-averse, cartoon characters make excellent endorsers, since the agency can pretty well control even Bart Simpson's behavior. Why we should listen to what a drawing on celluloid tells us is another question entirely.

But best of all are dead celebrities. They tell only the tales approved of by the executors of their estates. Since most of what a celebrity does is to attract attention, no one questions the inappropriateness of an impossible endorsement. Humphrey Bogart,

Marilyn Monroe, and even James Dean(!) magically appearing to tout Diet Coke is shocking enough; no one cares that the product was introduced long after their demise. And when The Gap ran a campaign in which Babe Ruth, Ernest Hemingway, and the same James Dean(!) were now endorsing khaki, who was disturbed by the fact that The Gap was not even incorporated until the 1960s? Indeed, as ads for *Rolling Stone* claim, "Perception Is Reality."

That's what makes Michael Jordan such a keeper to commercial interests. He knows that what he sells is not shoes, underwear, eyeglasses, cologne, breakfast cereal, long-distance phone service, or even the National Basketball Association. What he sells is perception, the perception of the brand Michael Jordan. He sells it so well that he was responsible for rocketing Nike from 18 percent of the sneaker market to 43 percent in just a decade. According to *Fortune* magazine, his glory flows deeper and farther than any other marketplace mortal. *Fortune* (June 22, 1998) figures his worth to Nike alone is $5.2 billion, and when you factor in his value—they call it the "Jordan effect"—elsewhere in commercial culture (to the NBA, to his other endorsements, to television, to his sports videos and movies . . .) he soon becomes the ten-billion-dollar man. And still counting. In Adland, no one jumps higher than that.

Works Cited

Archer, Gleason L. *History of Radio to 1926*. New York: American Historical Society, 1928.

Barnouw, Erik. *The Sponsor: Notes on a Modern Potentate*. New York: Oxford University Press, 1978.

Barnum, P. T. *The Life of P. T. Barnum, Written by Himself*. New York, Redfield, 1855.

Barton, Bruce. *The Man Nobody Knows: A Discovery of Jesus*. Indianapolis: Bobbs-Merrill, 1925.

Bloom, Harold. *The Anxiety of Influence: A Theory of Poetry*. New York: Oxford University Press, 1973.

Boorstin, Daniel J. "Advertising and American Civilization." In Yale Brozen, ed., *Advertising and Society*, 11–23. New York: New York University Press, 1974.

———. *The Americans: The Democratic Experience*. New York: Random House, 1973.

———. *The Image: A Guide to Pseudo-Events in America*. New York: Atheneum, 1961.

Brooks, Cleanth, and Robert Penn Warren. *Understanding Poetry*. 3rd edition. New York: Holt, Rinehart and Winston, 1960.

Burdan, Marshall, and Chris Meyer. "Flower Power: Twenty-Five Years Later." *Campaigns & Elections*, October 1989, 36–37.

Burnett, Leo. *100 Leo's: The Wit and Wisdom of Leo Burnett*. Lincolnwood, Ill.: NTC Business Books, 1995.

Burton, Jean. *Lydia Pinkham Is Her Name*. New York: Farrar, Straus and Company, 1949.

Calkins, Earnest Elmo. *And Hearing Not*. New York: Charles Scribner's Sons, 1946.

Carrier, Jim. "Death of a Salesman: Marlboro Man Bows Out." *The Denver Post*, August 26, 1996.

Colford, Steven W. "Spawned From a 'Daisy': Presidential TV Ads Have Addressed Issues, Set Emotional Tones, and Caused Controversy." *Advertising Age*, February 28, 1995, 46.

Danzig, Fred. "The Big Idea: Philip Morris and Marlboro." *Advertising Age*, November 9, 1988, 16.

Della Femina, Jerry. *From Those Wonderful Folks Who Gave You Pearl Harbor: Front-Line Dispatches from the Advertising War*. New York: Simon & Schuster, 1970.

Dempsey, Mike. *Bubbles: Early Advertising Art from A & F Pears*. London: Fontana, 1978.

Diamond, Edwin, and Stephen Bates. *The Spot: The Rise of Political Advertising in Television*. Cambridge, Mass.: MIT Press, 1984.

Dougherty, Philip H. "Defining a 'Charlie' for Revlon." *New York Times*, November 28, 1986.

Dyson, Paul, Andy Farr, and Nigel S. Hollis. "Understanding, Measuring, and Using Brand Equity." *Journal of Advertising Research*, November 21, 1996, 9ff.

Educational Services, *The Saturday Evening Post*. "Advertising Case History #8." Philadelphia: The Curtis Publishing Co., 1948.

Engel, Louis. *How to Buy Stocks*. 5th edition. New York: Bantam Books, 1972.

Ferguson, Andrew. "The Power of Myth: Bill Moyers, Liberal Fraud." *The New Republic*, August 19, 1991, 22ff.

Fox, Stephen. *The Mirror Makers: A History of American Advertising and Its Creators*. New York: William Morrow, 1984.

Frank, Thomas C. *The Conquest of Cool: Business Culture, Counterculture, and the Rise of Hip Consumerism*. Chicago: University of Chicago Press, 1997.

Frazer, James. *The Golden Bough: A Study in Magic and Religion*. Abridged edition, New York: Macmillan, 1922.

Fukuyama, Francis. "The End of History?" *The National Interest* 16 (1989), 3–18.

———. *The End of History and the Last Man*. New York: Free Press, 1992.

Galbraith, John Kenneth. *The Affluent Society*. Revised edition. Boston: Houghton Mifflin, 1969.

Gardner, Burleigh, and Sidney Levy. "The Product and the Brand." *Harvard Business Review* 33, no. 2 (1955), 33–39.

Garfield, Bob. "In Defense of Commercials." *Advertising Age*, February 28, 1995, 24.

Goldberg, Fred. "Recalling *1984* Spot." *Advertising Age*, January 31, 1994, 21.

Gossage, Howard. *Is There Any Hope for Advertising?* Urbana, Ill.: University of Illinois Press, 1986.

Hall, Jane. "Bill Moyers Holds a Mirror Up to America." *Los Angeles Times*, November 12, 1989, 4.

Hall, Steve. "Packaging Politicians for TV." *Indianapolis Star*, September 6, 1996.

Hampel, Alvin. "Fear: the Ultimate Creative Motivator." *Advertising Age*, January 1, 1988, 25.

Hawthorne, Timothy R. *The Complete Guide to Infomercial Marketing*. Lincolnwood, Ill.: NTC Business Books, 1997.

Hine, Thomas. *The Total Package: The Secret History and Hidden Meanings of Boxes, Bottles, Cans, and Other Persuasive Containers*. New York: Little Brown, 1995.

Hirsch, E. D., Jr. *Cultural Literacy: What Every American Needs to Know*. Boston: Houghton Mifflin, 1987.

Hixon, Carl. "The Bernbach Fantasies." *Advertising Age*, August 11, 1986, 24.

Hopkins, Claude C. *My Life in Advertising & Scientific Advertising*. 1923, 1927, Rpt. Lincolnwood, Ill.: NTC Business Books, 1991.

Huxley, Aldous. "Advertisement." In *Essays Old and New*, 126–131. New York: Harper & Row, 1968.

Jackman, Michael. *Crown's Book of Political Quotations*. New York: Crown, 1982.

James, Clive. *Fame in the Twentieth Century*. New York: Random House, 1993.

Johnson, Bradley. "10 Years After *1984*." *Advertising Age*, January 10, 1994, 1.

Johnson, Roy S. "The Jordan Effect." *Fortune*, June 22, 1998, 124ff.

Kanner, Bernice. *The 100 Best TV Commercials*. New York: Times Business, 1999.

Keats, John. *The Insolent Chariots*. Philadelphia: Lippincott, 1958.

Kroll, Jack. "Jingles and Singles." *Newsweek*, March 31, 1975, 69.

Kunhardt, Philip B., Jr., Philip B. Kunhardt III, and Peter W. Kunhardt. *P. T. Barnum: America's Greatest Showman*. New York: Knopf, 1995.

Lambert, Gerard. *All Out of Step: A Personal Chronicle*. New York: Doubleday, 1956.

———. "How I Sold Listerine." In Editors of *Fortune*, eds., *The Amazing Advertising Business*, 49–59. New York: Simon & Schuster, 1957.

Leach, Ken. *Perfume Presentation: 100 Years of Artistry*. Toronto: Kres Publishing, 1997.

Levenson, Bob. *Bill Bernbach's Book: A History of the Advertising That Changed the History of Advertising*. New York: Villard, 1987.

Lewis, Richard W. *Absolut Book: The Absolut Vodka Advertising Story*. Boston: Journey Editions, 1996.

Mann, Charles C., and Mark L. Plummer. *The Aspirin Wars*. New York: Knopf, 1991.

Marchand, Roland. *Advertising the American Dream: Making Way for Modernity, 1920–1940*. Berkeley: University of California Press, 1985.

McConnell, Frank. "Truly Dishonest, and Joe Six-Pack Knows It." *Commonweal*, January 29, 1993, 14ff.

McGuire, John M. "How the Marlboro Cowboy Acquired His Tattoo." *St. Louis Post-Dispatch*, November 12, 1989.

Metcalf, Nelson, Jr. "Writer Recalls Famed World War II Ad." *Advertising Age*, June 3, 1991, 24.

Morgan, David, ed. *Icons of American Protestantism: The Art of Warner Sallman*. New Haven: Yale University Press, 1996.

Ogilvy, David. *Confessions of an Advertising Man*. New York: Atheneum, 1963.

———. *On Advertising*. New York: Vintage, 1985.

Packard, Vance. *The Hidden Persuaders*. New York: McKay, 1956.

Polykoff, Shirley. *Does She . . . Or Doesn't She?: And How She Did It*. New York: Doubleday, 1975.

Reed, John. *Ten Days That Shook the World*. New York: Boni and Liveright, 1919.

Reeves, Rosser. *Reality in Advertising*. New York: Knopf, 1961.

Rothenberg, Randall. *Where the Suckers Moon: An Advertising Story*. New York: Knopf, 1994.

Rowsome, Frank. *They Laughed When I Sat Down: An Informal History of Advertising*. New York: Bonanza Books, 1959.

Saxon, A. H. *P. T. Barnum: The Legend and the Man*. New York: Columbia University Press, 1989.

Schofield, Perry, ed. *100 Top Copy Writers and Their Favorite Ads*. New York: Printer's Ink Publishing Company, 1954.

Simpson, James B. *Contemporary Quotations*. New York: Crowell, 1964.

Sundblom, Haddon H. *Dream of Santa: Haddon Sundblom's Vision*. Washington, D.C.: Staples & Charles, 1992.

Tocqueville, Alexis de. *Democracy in America*. New York: Knopf, 1994.

Turner, E. S. *The Shocking History of Advertising*. New York: E. P. Dutton, 1953.

Twitchell, James B. *Adcult: The Triumph of Advertising in American Culture*. New York: Columbia University Press, 1955.

Vanden Bergh, Bruce G. "The Bug with Chutzpah." *WorldPaper*, April 1993, 8.

Wakeman, Frederic. *The Hucksters*. New York: Rinehart & Co., 1946.

Watkins, Julian. *The 100 Greatest Advertisements: Who Wrote Them and What They Did*. New York: Moore, 1949.

Weber, Max. *The Protestant Ethic and the Spirit of Capitalism*. Translated by Talcott Parsons. 1905. Reprint, New York: Scribner, 1958.

Whiteside, Thomas. "Annals of Television: The Man from Iron City." *The New Yorker*, September 27, 1969, 47ff.

Will, George. "The Real Game: The Commercials." *Washington Post*, January 28, 1990.

Williams, Raymond. "The Magic System." *New Left Review* 4 (1960), 27–32.

Index

Absolut vodka, 174–83
Abstract Expressionism, 7
Adbusters, 182–83
Ad Council, 82, 83–84
Addiction, selling of, 126–35
Addie Awards, 8
Ad Track, 174
Advertising:
  advocacy, 80–87
  altruistic, 54
  anonymous, 108
  as art form, 4–5, 7–9
  brand built by, 211
  category, 95–96
  as commercial speech, 1–4
  courses in, 4
  effectiveness of, 3, 7–8, 80, 133
  event, 20, 193
  forgettable, 5–6, 8
  immediacy of, 3, 5–6
  importance of, 8
  innovations in, 80
  issue, 83
  line between art and, 45–47
  lists of, 6–7
  meaning added via, 10–13, 38
  music and, 46, 77, 203
  negative, 154–61
  political, 154–61
  power of, 9–15
  pro bono, 82
  profound, 7
  programming separate from, 198, 200
  religion and, 11–12, 23
  spending and revenues in, 24
  testing of, 67–69
  tradition of, 4–9
  war and, 82–87

Advertising Age, 6, 7, 112–13, 189
Advertorials, 203
Advocacy advertising, 80–87
Ailes, Roger, 161
Air Jordan, 204–15
Alcohol advertising, 177–83
Alka-Seltzer, 3
Allen, Woody, 113, 193
American Home Products, 151
American Museum, 19, 21
American Revolution, 13
Amos 'n' Andy (hit radio show), 78
Anacin, 146–53
Apple Computer, 184–93
Aquavit, 176
Armani, Giorgio, 171
Aromatherapy, 167
Arrow Collar Man, 139–40
Art:
  advertising as form of, 4–5, 7–9
  and associated value, 40, 43
  and commerce, 46–47, 88, 96
  line between advertising and, 45–47
  modern, 7
  museums, 193
  Pop, 47, 181–82
  as propaganda, 9
  Renaissance, 7, 47
  repetition and value of, 44
  taste and, 43
Artforum, 176
Aspirin, 146–53
Association, power of, 42, 52
AT&T, 75–76, 78, 93–94, 193, 195
Auden, W. H., 157
Audience:
  creation of, 20
  demographics of, 196

Audience: *(cont.)*
   getting the attention of, 7
   niche, 34
Automobile ads, 114–17
Autry, Gene, 106
Ayer, F. W., 23, 93
Ayer, N. W., & Son, 34, 88, 93–96
Aykroyd, Dan, 202–3

Bachelor cards, 30
Ballyhoo, use of term, 21
Bankhead, Tallulah, 21
Barnum, P. T., 16–25, 40, 117
Barratt, Thomas J., 38, 40–47, 139, 181
Barth, John, 116
Barton, Bruce, 23
Basketball players, 204–9
Bates, Ted, Agency, 149, 150
Bayer aspirin, 146–47, 151, 152
Beecher, Henry Ward, 42
Benny, Jack, 198
Bergerac, Michel, 172
Bernbach, William, 108, 110–17, 153
Berra, Yogi, 191–92, 211
Billboards, television, 196
Bissell carpet sweepers, 50
Blackwell, M. H., 70–74, 78–79
Blockbuster, 78
Bloom, Harold, 108, 112
Body odor, 62
Bogart, Humphrey, 214–15
Boorstin, Daniel, 14
Booty pat, 163, 170, 173
Boston Tea Party, 13
Bowerman, Bill, 209
Boy's Life magazine, 206
Bradley, Carl "Big-un," 131
Brand extensions, 124–25, 133–34, 144, 172
Branding:
   defined, 136
   designer, 145, 170–71
   personalities, 138–42, 171, 204–15
   purpose of, 135, 211
   uses of term, 138, 143–44
Brecht, Bertolt, 116
Bricolage, 208
Bristol-Myers, 151

Broadcasting, 70–79
Brooks, Cleanth, 8
Bubbles (A Child's World) (Millais), 43–47, 181
Bufferin, 151, 152
Bunkum, use of term, 21
Burnett, Leo, 55–56, 129–33
Bush, George, 156
Buy-hole, 92

Cable channels, 203
Calendar cards, 30
Calkins, Earnest Elmo, 6
Campbell, Catherine, 171
Cannes International Advertising
   Film Festival, 189
Canon, 38, 40
Capitalism, ads as art of, 4–5, 7–9
Cassini, Oleg, 170
Category advertising, 95–96
Celebrities, over-the-hill, 202
Celebrity endorsements, 25, 42, 211–15
Celebrity scent, 171
Chanel, Coco, 167, 170
Chaplin, Charlie, 113, 190
Charlie, 162–73
Chiat/Day, 187, 189, 192
Christmas, 102–7
Christmas cards, 30, 105
Chromolithography (chromos), 29, 43, 105
Cigarettes, 126–35
Cikovsky, Nicolia, 88
Claptrap, use of term, 21
Cleveland, Grover, 154
Clio Awards, 8
Coca-Cola, 102–7, 180, 215
Codswallop, use of term, 21
Color Research Institute, 132
Commerce:
   and art, 46–47, 88, 96
   clichés of, 5
   language of, 1–4
   religion and, 11–12, 13, 14–15
Commercialism, 13, 15, 25
   defined, 10, 38
   separate from programming, 198, 200
Commodification, 11, 14
Communications Act (1934), 75

Confessions of an Advertising Man
    (Ogilvy), 141
Constructive discontent, 60, 62, 68
Consumer-based positioning, 68–69, 131–32
Consumption:
    cathedrals of, 13
    conspicuous, 10
    meanings of, 8, 38
    and redemption, 25
Copy:
    ambiguous, 123–25
    body, 142–43
    for female readers, 96–99
Copyright, lack of, 36, 132
Corelli, Marie, 45
Coupons, 53, 55, 67–69, 195
Creativity, 7, 8–9, 26
Crocker, Betty, 37
Crockett, Davy, 21
Cronkite, Walter, 149
Cubism, 7
Culkin, Macaulay, 214
Cultural Literacy (Hirsch), 184–86
Culture:
    commercial, 1 4, 5, 185
    disposable, 3
    global, 15
    high, 43
    popular, 146, 184–86, 193
Curtis, Cyris, 72

"Daisy," 154–61
Daniels, Draper, 130
Davis, Elmer, 87
DDB (Doyle Dane Bernbach Inc.), 111, 114, 155,
    158–60
Dean, James, 215
De Beers Consolidated Mines Ltd., 88–101
Della Famina, Jerry, 112
Designer brands, 145, 170–71
Desire, creation of, 5, 8, 15
Diamonds, 88–101
Dickens, Charles, 48
Diddley, Bo, 212
Dior, Christian, 167, 170
Direct marketing, 35
Direct-transaction business, 203

Disease, germ theory of, 54–55
Disney Company, 106
Dole, Bob, 160
Doner, W. B. & Co., 107
Doyle Dane Bernbach Inc. (DDB), 111, 114,
    155, 158–60
Dream, selling, 18
Drinking songs, 36
Dr. Kilmer and Company Standard
    Herbal Remedies, 28
DRTV (direct-response television), 202
Drummers (salesmen), 30
Dukakis, Michael, 156
Dusenberry, Phil, 156

Economic depression, 82
Education, compulsory, 38
Effie Awards, 8
Ehrlich, Aaron, 158
800 numbers, 195
El Al, 111
Elephants:
    Jumbo, 10, 20
    white, 19–20
Elvis brands, 59
Endorsements:
    by cartoon characters, 214
    celebrity, 25, 42, 211–15
Eng and Chang (Siamese twins), 21
Entertainment Weekly, 6–7, 189
Estes, Lydia, 32
Ether advertising, 75–76
Ethical drug manufacturers, 31
Event advertising, 20, 193
Events, media-made (pseudo), 20, 21, 24,
    25, 188–93
Excedrin headaches, 152
Exchanges, network of, 11
Exvertisement, 80, 83

Fame in the Twentieth Century (James), 213
FCC (Federal Communications Commission),
    75, 197, 198, 202
Feasley, Milton, 60
Filmation Associates, 109

Flimflam, use of term, 21
FMCGs (fast-moving consumer goods), 51–52
Food and Drug Administration, 153
Foote, Cone & Belding, 120–23
Forbes, 135
Ford, Henry, 116
Fortune, 215
Fowler, Mark, 198
Fragrance abuse, 162, 164
Frankenheimer, John, 193
Frankenstein (film), 156–57
Frazer, Sir James, 57
Freedom, meanings of, 13–14
French Revolution, 15
Friedan, Betty, 120
Fuessle, Milton, 64, 65
Fukuyama, Francis, 15
Fungibility, 10, 11

Gallup, George, 68, 139
Gamble, James, 41
Gap, The, 215
Gardner, Burleigh, 144
Garfield, Bob, 6
Garner, James, 37, 214
Gear Without Limits, 133–34
Gelb, Lawrence M., 120
Gender, use of, 190
Generation X, 2, 117, 164
Georgi, Ed, 84
Gerety, Frances, 98
Ghost brands, 59
Gianninoto, Frank, 131
Gillette, 124
Giotto, 7
Girlie calendars, 30
Godard, Jean-Luc, 193
Godfrey, Arthur, 198
Goldwater, Barry, 156, 158–59
Gone With the Wind (film), 149
Good Housekeeping, 121
Goodyear tires, 51
Gorgeous George, 118
Gossage, Howard, 108, 110
Grant, Ulysses S., 24, 154
Grey Advertising, 110–12

Halitosis, 60, 64–65
Hall, Jane, 159–60
Halloween, 102, 104
Halo, 178–80
Harlow, Jean, 118
Harper's, 176
Harvard Business Review, 144
Hatfield, Henry, 78
Hathaway man, 136–45
Hathaway Shirt Company, 139, 140–41
Hawthorne, Nathaniel, 70–71
Hayes, Geoff, 180
Head of Christ (Sallman), 86, 87
Heath, Joice, 21
Helmsley, Leona, 37
Hemingway, Ernest, 16, 215
Hilfiger, Tommy, 171
Hine, Thomas, 177
Hippocrates, 146
Hirsch, E. D., 184
History:
    culture vs., 3–4
    end of, 15
    memory and, 3
Hit shows, nationwide radio, 78
Holidays, 102–7
Home-shopping networks, 203
Hoopla, use of term, 21
Hoover, Herbert, 72
Hopkins, Claude, 23, 48, 50–58, 110, 150, 195
Huckleberry Finn (Twain), 17
Hucksters, The (Wakeman), 110
Humbug, use of term, 21, 22
Huxley, Aldous, 9
Hype, 21, 22, 25, 34, 40

Iacocca, Lee, 37
IBM, 190, 192
Iconoclasm, 182
Illustrated London News, 43–44
Images, power of, 19, 187–88
Impressionism, 7, 44
Incense, defined, 167
Industrial Revolution, 9–10, 138
Infomercials, 194–203

Ingram, Sir William, 43, 44
Inks, colored, 29
Internet advertising, 73, 79
Issue advertising, 83

J

Jackson, Andrew, 154
Jackson, Bo, 212
James, Clive, 213
James, Adm. Sir William, 43
Jefferson, Thomas, 154
Jetté, Edith, 140–41
Jetté, Ellerton, 141, 144
Jobs, Steve, 189
John Scudder's American Museum, 19
Johnson, Lyndon B., 154–61
Johnson, Samuel, 16
Johnson & Johnson, 152
Jo-Jo the Dog-Faced Boy, 22
Jokes and songs, 34, 36
Jordan, Michael, 37, 42, 204–15
Jorgenson, George, 129–30
Jumbomania, 19, 20

K

Kanner, Bernice, 6
Karloff, Boris, 156
Keaton, Buster, 113
Khrushchev, Nikita, 150
Kid in Upper 4, The, 80–87
Kiss, in courtship, 165–66, 170
Klein, Calvin, 168, 171
Knight, Phil, 209–11
Koenig, Julian, 114
Kris Kringle, 104
Kroll, Jack, 5
Krone, Helmut, 114

L

Lacroix, Christian, 170
Lambert, Gerard, 60, 63–65, 67–69
Lambert, Jordan Wheat, 62–63
Langtry, Lily, 42
Language, uses of, 1–4, 21, 22, 25
Lauren, Ralph, 171

Leacock, Stephen, 5
Leavis, F. R., 5
Lee, Spike, 193, 209
Leonardo da Vinci, 7
Levenson, Bob, 111
Lever Brothers, 58–59, 88
Leverhume, Lord, 8, 88
Levy, Sidney, 144
Levy's bread, 111
Lewis, Richard, 180, 181
Leyendecker, J. C., 139
Life, 123, 132
Lilly, Eli, 31
Lincoln, Abraham, 154
Lipton Tea, 198
Lister, Joseph, 62–63
Listerine, 60–69
Lithography, 29
Lois, George, 14
Long, C. H., 131
L'Oreal, 125, 214
Loren, Sophia, 171
Lorimar Telepictures, 199–200
Lottery tickets, sale of, 18
Louis-Dreyfus, Julia, 125
Lucky Strike cigarettes, 34, 52
Lyden, John, 150
Lynch, David, 193

M

McCarthy, Eugene, 156
McCombe, Leonard, 131
McDonald, Ronald, 37
MacDougall, Mal, 171
Machine age, 10, 38
Machine made things, value added to, 10–11, 13, 38
Macintosh computers, 186–87, 192
McLuhan, Marshall, 4
MacManus, Theodore, 23
Magazine advertising, 72–73, 162, 164, 174–83
    advertorials, 203
    collectors of, 176
    outserts, 203
Magazines, picture, 43
Magic, power of, 55–59
Maher, Bill, 192

Marketing, 11
  direct, 35
  importance of, 147–48
  long-form, 202
  relationship, 35
Marketing plans, 34
Market research, 68, 126, 128, 129,
    131–32, 139
Marlboro Man, 37, 126–35
Marx, Karl, 10, 15
Mass production, 136
Materialism, 9–10
Maximilian, Archduke of Austria, 91
May, Robert L., 107
Media, 70–79, 146–49, 194–203
Memories, institutional, 3
Metcalf, Nelson, Jr., 80, 84–86
Metonymy, 134
MGM, 149
Michelangelo, 7, 47
Miles, Michael, 134, 135
Millais, John E., 38, 43, 45
Miss Clairol, 37, 118–25
Mr. Clean, 37
Mob, use of term, 38, 41
Monopolies, laws against, 93, 94
Monroe, Marilyn, 171, 215
Montgomery Ward, 107
Moore, Clement Clarke, 104–5
Moyers, Bill, 159–60
Multinational companies, 167–68
Music, 46, 77
Music videos, 203
My Life in Advertising (Hopkins), 48

Naming the product, 168–69
Napoleon Bonaparte, 15
Nast, Thomas, 104, 105
Nation, Carry, 32
Nation, The, 20, 22–23
NEA (National Education Association), 78
Negative advertising, 154–61
Network broadcasting, 77
New Haven Railroad, 80, 83, 84–87
Newspaper inserts, 34, 43
Newsweek, 5
New York, 176

New Yorker, The, 136, 139, 149, 164, 176, 181
New York Herald, 42
New York Sun, 21
New York Times, The, 170, 191
Nielsen ratings, 43
Nike, 204–15
Nimbus (halo), 178–80
1984 (Apple ad), 184–93
1984 (Orwell), 186
Nixon, Richard M., 161
Noses, 164
Notes, in smells, 165

Ogilvy, David, 48, 110, 126, 129, 136–45, 153
Olivier, Sir Laurence, 2
Olympic Games, 213–14
Opinion surveys, 68
Oppenheimer, Ernest, 93
Orbach's, 111
Orwell, George, 9, 185–86
Outserts, 203

Packaging, 131–32, 177–83
Pain medication, 146–53
Paley, William, 77
Palmolive soap, 51, 56
Parity items, 10, 118, 138
Patent:
  loss of, 147
  use of term, 26
Patent medicine ads, 26–37
Pears, Andrew, 41
Pears' Soap, 38–47, 181
Pepsi, 156
Pepsodent toothpaste, 48–59, 78
Perception, selling of, 215
Perdue, Frank, 37
Perfume:
  advertising, 162–73
  bottles for, 177–78
  defined, 167
  elevator emptiers, 172
  naming of, 168–69
Phelps, William Lyon, 17
Philip Morris Company, 129–35

Phillips, Irna, 197
Photolithography, 43
Picasso, Pablo, 48, 143
Pinkham, Dan, 33–34
Pinkham, Isaac, 32
Pinkham, Lydia E.,
      Vegetable Compound, 26–37
Pitch, delivery of, 20
Pitchmen, 22
Placebo, and hype, 34
Playboy, 176
Poe, Edgar Allan, 21
Poetry, 8
Political advertising, 154–61
Polykoff, Shirley, 121–23
Pond's Vanishing Cream, 41
Pop art, 47, 181–82
Positioning, 41–42, 50, 68–69, 148
Powers, John E., 3
Prang, Louis, 105
Preemptive claims for products, 50–53
Prentis, Lou, 106
Pre-Raphaelite Brotherhood, 43
Presley, Elvis, 48
Prices, inelastic, 135
Printers' Ink, 6
Pro bono advertising, 82
Procter & Gamble, 69
Product:
    as by-product of advertising, 211
    ghost brands, 59
    hero as, 204–15
    interchangeability of, 51, 52
    naming of, 168–69
    parity, 10, 118, 138
    placement of, 34
    preemptive claims for, 50–53
    selling need vs., 60
    surpluses of, 80
Prolepsis, 116
Propaganda, art as, 9
Proselytizing, 11
Prostitutes, 118, 120
*Protestant Ethic and the Spirit of Capitalism,
      The* (Weber), 11
Protestant Reformation, 11
Proust, Marcel, 164
Prudential Insurance, 90
Pseudo-events, 20, 21, 24, 25, 188–93

Public broadcasting, 78
Pytka, Joe, 208

Quaker Oats, 51
Queensboro Corporation, 70–73

Radio advertising, 70–79, 82, 83, 148, 197
Rankin, William, 76
RCA (Radio Corporation of America), 74
Reagan, Ronald, 140, 156, 190, 198
Reality in Advertising (Reeves), 150
Reebok, 208
Reed, John, 9
Reeves, Rosser, 11, 110, 147, 149–50, 153, 160
Religion:
    advertising in, 11–12, 23
    commerce and, 11–12, 13, 14–15
    magic and, 56
    as popular culture, 146
Renaissance art, 7, 47
Repetition, power of, 44, 150
Research, market, 68, 126, 128, 129, 131–32, 139
Revlon, 169, 172
Revson, Charles, 169
Reynolds, R. J., Co., 129
Rhodes, Cecil, 94
Richardson, Lunsford, 31
Riney, Hal, 156
Riswold, Jim, 211
Rockefeller, Nelson, 159
Rock of Ages Corporation, 88, 90
Rock of Gibraltar, 90
Rockwell, Norman, 58, 84
Roper, Elmo & Associates, 131–32
Roux, Michel, 180–82
Rudolph the Red-Nosed Reindeer, 107
Ruth, Babe, 215

Saint Nicholas, 104
Sallman, Warner, 86
Santa Claus, 102–7
Sara Lee Corp., 144
Saturday Evening Post, 72–73, 97, 106

Saturday Night Fever (film), 2
Saturday Night Live, 202–3
Scent strips, 162, 164
Schlitz beer, 51
Schwartz, Tony, 158, 159, 160
Schweppes, Commander, 141
Scott, Ridley, 187–88, 193
Scott Toilet Tissue, 3
Seagrove, Gordon, 64, 65
Sell-through, 133–34
Selznick, David O., 149
Sententiae, 5
Sex appeal, 55, 58, 165–67
Sex-change operations, 129–30
Shakespeare, William, 17, 19, 26, 174
Shepherd, Cybill, 214
Show business, early, 19
Siamese twins, Eng and Chang, 21
Simpson, O.J., 37, 214
Slogans, 46, 58, 65–67, 83, 93, 99, 121–23,
    172, 213
  for brand extensions, 124–25
  positioning via, 41–42
Smell, sense of, 164–67
Smirnoff vodka, 182, 183
Soap, 40–47, 63
Soap operas, 197
Soloflex, 200
Songs and jokes, 34, 36
Spokespersons, 37
Spontaneous trait transference, 211
Sprewell, Latrell, 213
Sterling Winthrop, 151
Stratton, Charles (Tom Thumb), 21
Stuart, John, 139
Sublime, 204
Sumptuary laws, 91
Sundblom, Haddon H., 106, 107
Super Bowl, 190–92
Supply and demand, 90–91, 92
Swift & Company Cotosuet shortening, 50–51
Syncretism, 102

Tarantino, Quentin, 108
TBWA, 180
Telemarketers, 196
Television, 76, 79, 82, 133, 148, 206–7

barter syndication, 199–200
channel stoppers, 202
infomercials, 194–203
remote clicker and, 153, 201
two-thirds rule in, 201
Ten Days That Shook the World (Reed), 9
Tetley Tea, 52
Thompson, J. Walter, Agency, 90, 96
Threes, power of, 151
Thumb, Gen. Tom (Stratton), 21
Tocqueville, Alexis de, 13–14
Today's Children (soap opera), 197
Toll broadcasting, 75
Toothpaste, 53–59
Toy-based shows, 199–200
Trade cards, 29–35
  collectors of, 30
  for Lydia Pinkham Compound, 31–35
  as stiffeners, 30
  verso text of, 29, 31
Travolta, John, 2
Trial-size products, 34, 42
Truman, Harry S, 82
Turner, Ted, 145
Twain, Mark, 17
Tylenol, 152

Understanding Poetry (Brooks and Warren), 8
Unique Selling Proposal, 150, 153
Universities of the Air, 76–78
USA Today, 191

Value:
  added, 10–11, 13, 38
  associated, 40, 43, 47, 95
  commodification and, 11, 14
  creation of, 11, 18, 25
  exchange, 10
  flow of, 213
  Jordan effect, 215
  use vs. prestige, 10
  yearning for objects of, 183
VanCamp pork and beans, 51
Van Heusen shirts, 140
Verso text, 29, 31

Video Storyboard, 5–6
Vodka, 174–83
Voice of Authority, 148–49
Volkswagen Beetle, 108–17

W

Wagner, Robert, 78
Wakeman, Frederic, 110
Wall Street Journal, The, 191
Wanamaker, John, 8, 88
Wanamaker's department store, 3
War, and advertising, 82–87
War Advertising Council, 82–83
Ward, Artemas, 23
Warhol, Andy, 47, 181
Warner-Lambert, 69
Warren, Robert Penn, 8
Watkins, Julian Lewis, 6
WATS numbers, 195
Weber, Max, 11
Weiden, Dan, 209, 210, 211
Weiden & Kennedy, 204, 209–12
Wellcome, Henry, 31
Westinghouse Corporation, 74

Whale, James, 156
Whisper copy, 67
Wild Men of Borneo, 22
Willis, Bruce, 214
Wilson, Jerry, 200
Winston cigarettes, 128
Women's movement, 118, 120, 123, 125,
    169–73, 190
Wonder Bread, 52
World War I, 74, 82
World War II, 78, 82
World Wide Web, interactive buying on, 203
Wozniak, Steve, 188–89
Wrangell, Baron George, 136, 137, 140–42

Y

Young, James Webb, 23
Young, Robert, 37

Z

Zinc plates, 29